God Uses Ordinary People

God Uses Ordinary People

A Memoir of Church Planting

Edna Bright

PROVIDENCE HOUSE PUBLISHERS
Franklin, Tennessee

Printed in the United States of America

02   01   00   99   98   1   2   3   4   5

Library of Congress Catalog Card Number: 98-67738

ISBN: 1-57736-117-2

Cover design by Gary Bozeman

PROVIDENCE HOUSE PUBLISHERS
238 Seaboard Lane • Franklin, Tennessee 37067
800-321-5692

To the memory of Cornelius Bright

In honor of Alona and June

To the memory and honor of the hundreds of people
who helped us start churches

Contents

Preface

HOW AND WHEN ONE COMES TO KNOW GOD'S WILL for his life is not spelled out anywhere in words, and we can't just read the Bible and know. However, once we accept Christ as Savior (the starting point) we learn to live in tune with God and become sensitive to his leadership. Then, when the "call" comes, the heart is ready to receive and respond to it.

Cornelius and I looked upon our families and early childhood experiences as influences that led us to a time of commitment, not just to each other in marriage, but, also, to a higher call on our lives because we were Christians.

We could not possibly know all we would encounter (the places we'd live, the jobs we'd hold, the people we'd come to know) before we finally knew, without a doubt, that God wanted us to start churches. It was through the years we went to school, the churches we belonged to and worked in, and all the people with spiritual needs we met that God led us step-by-step to prepare us for what he eventually called us to do.

Neither of our families understood our call or our commitment to it. They believed we could/should serve God and minister to people in Alabama, where they lived, instead of going way off, up north. They loved us and prayed for us, but they did not truly understand.

However, families and friends weren't responsible for our call. They didn't know what God was leading us to do. We learned, early on, that we were accountable to God alone, and we served him in that realization, wherever he led us. God continually blessed us with people and opportunities that increased our awareness of the spiritual needs of our nation. Our call was to help meet those needs by sharing Christ and congregationalizing those who believed.

I wrote GOD USES ORDINARY PEOPLE as a memoir of the joyous years we spent living in his presence and following his will. My prayer is that all who read this book will sense, as we did, that God uses all of his people who make themselves available to him.

Great joy and contentment is found as one travels that road.

CHAPTER 1

Country Boy Meets City/Country Girl

LIFE STARTS SOMEWHERE FOR EVERYBODY. IT STARTED for us in the deep South. Cornelius and I were products of rural north Alabama. However, he was born in Bartow County, Georgia, on March 14, 1919, to Thomas Henry and Ida Forsyth Bright. He was the seventh of eleven children born in this order: Roda Lee, Thomas Cara, Sanford Wilson, Jossie Rean, Gordon Raymond, Etta, Cornelius, Cecil, Magdalene, Phillip Aldon, and Roberta.

Three of the children, Jossie Rean, age five; Cecil, age one; and Etta, age twelve, died in childhood and left a deep hole, emotionally, in the family. The others lived to maturity and even to old age.

The T. H. Bright family farmed for a living. Mr. Bright was also a preacher. They moved from Georgia around 1922 to a farm near Ragland, Alabama. That was where the tragedy of Etta's death took place. She was burned to death while spending the night, Christmas Eve, with a friend. Having already lost Jossie Rean and Cecil to childhood diseases, this was an especially hard blow for the family.

When the boys were old enough to make the crops, Mr. Bright often left the farming to them. He would preach revivals

1

and attend protracted meetings. Through the years he was pastor of more than sixteen churches.

The family moved to St. Clair County, Alabama, in 1927. As the custom was, farmers moved every year or two. Following that custom, the Bright family moved again in 1929, this time to Marshall County, Alabama, where they settled on Sand Mountain in the High Point Community. They liked that area and stayed there about six years.

The next move brought a wonderful time in Cornelius's life. The family moved to Whitesville where Cornelius met and fell in love with Dorothy Walden. He was sixteen, and she was fifteen. She was a sweet, willowy blond who enjoyed playing tennis. The Brights wanted Cornelius to pay more attention to farming, and less to tennis, but he and Dorothy loved the game and played every chance they got. Cornelius remembered his first love with fondness, and, years later when I met Dorothy, I found her to be a fine Christian lady. She and I became good friends.

The family began shrinking because Roda, Cara, and Sanford had married and moved away from home. The family moved once more, this time to Geraldine, Alabama. It was in 1936. And, that's the year Cornelius became a confirmed bachelor, at the ripe old age of seventeen. He missed Dorothy and tennis very much. He and his best friend, Oel Hendrix, often talked of bachelorhood. Both vowed that would be their lot. (But no, it didn't work for Oel either.) The Bright family lived at Geraldine when I met Cornelius in 1938.

Now begins my side of the story. I was born August 7, 1923, near Albertville, Alabama, in Marshall County. I was the fourth of seven children born to John Rance and Alma Cook Smith in this order: Robert Christi, Chester Roland, Nina Vae, Edna Marvell, Mildred Mae, Betty Marie, and a miscarried baby girl who lived only a few hours.

Grandpa and Grandma Smith lived with us. Grandpa died when we lived on South Broad Street in Albertville. That was in 1928. Daddy was a bookkeeper in town, but the crash in 1929 sent us scurrying back to the family farm down in the cove on Slab Creek. We were fortunate to have the farm to go to.

Those were good days for me because I loved the freedom on the farm. And I loved Pine Grove School where Mr. M. A. Brown and Mrs. Gladys Hale Downs were my teachers. I learned some important lessons in that little country school that stayed with me throughout my educational journey. I am sure that's where my dream to become a teacher was born. I never forgot Mr. Brown telling us we could be whatever we wanted to be, if we'd work for it. We believed him and worked hard. Well, at least some of us did.

I'll never forget Mr. Brown's great disappointment in a bunch of us who walked home together. For absolutely no reason, we decided to pull up Mr. Landers's turnips and eat them. That wasn't so bad, and Mr. Landers wouldn't have cared, if that had been all we'd done. But the older boys and girls pulled up many more turnips than we ate and just tossed them into the ditch.

Needless to say, we caught it when we got home. News traveled fast! I guess every parent spanked their involved children. I know Daddy did us. And the next day at school, Mr. Brown gave the bigger kids a good paddling. I happened to be one of the younger, smaller ones so I didn't get that paddling. However, I still felt guilty because I ate some of the turnips. I felt shame that we had disappointed Mr. Brown. We never got in the turnip patch again.

Looking back on those years I know I was happy, but it must have been a hard time for Mother and Daddy. Six children to feed and clothe, and another on the way, had to be stressful for them. Grandma was still with us, making nine mouths to feed. It had to be a challenge in those lean depression years.

The next three or four years were even harder. During that time our barn burned, killing most of our livestock and destroying all our feedstock. One milk cow was saved, but even she had a burned back that needed constant care and attention. Grandma Smith died, and Mother miscarried in her seventh month. She was precariously ill for many months afterwards.

I was nearly eight years old. I'd noticed Mother was getting fat, but I didn't know a baby was on the way. No one talked of such things. One Sunday morning, Daddy, unexpectedly, told us three older girls we could go spend the day with friends up the road about two miles. We were Nina, age ten; Edna, age eight; and Mildred, age six. Betty, the baby, was three, so she stayed home with relatives who had come in. We were so thrilled to go visiting we never questioned our good luck. We simply took off.

When we returned home late that afternoon, we discovered Mother was very sick, and the surprise baby was barely alive. I remember looking longingly at that pink bundle. Mildred was the only one of us who got to hold her. We girls were devastated! Our brothers, older than we, busied themselves outside—at the barn—but sorrow deepened inside the house. Relatives spoke tenderly to us of Mother's impending death. They hugged us and cried with us. We girls went to Mother's bed and begged her not to die. We told her we had named the baby "Ollie Jean," after her best friend.

Mother lived, thank God, but hers was a long, hard journey back to health. I am convinced that God saw our plight and, in his mercy, raised Mother up. How thankful we were!

We girls had to take on chores we'd never done before: washing, ironing, cooking, cleaning. Those were difficult times, not just for us girls, but for Daddy and the boys as they farmed. Crops weren't always good, and farm prices were often low. Daddy's World War I wounds left him not strong, and, though the boys were good workers, Daddy knew our future was not to be on the farm.

When Daddy got a job in town, we moved back to Albertville. That was in 1934, and I was in the seventh grade. We left R. C. and his bride, Eloise Boen, to work the farm. I remember we went down to help them for a couple of years during the hoeing and cotton-picking seasons. In retrospect, I'm not sure how much help we were.

My junior high years at Albertville were uneventful. I remember being with my friends and having fun but not studying a lot. But in high school, it was different. I began to enjoy studying and making good grades. I was on the debating team and took courses to prepare me for college. I remembered, during that time, Mr. Brown's advice at Pine Grove School: "You can be whatever you're willing to work for, to make it happen."

In memory those fun years were full of excitement. My friends were very important to me. We dated in groups, seldom singling out partners. School work was important, and most of us applied ourselves to our studies. However, we lived for the weekends. We always had something planned, and we all participated. We'd have a wiener roast in a pasture, a party at someone's home, or go to a movie, cave exploring, hiking, swimming, dancing, and ball games. Few cars among us meant most of our fun was had close to home. It was never dull, and we never ran out of ideas. (I wonder why young people don't have anything to do today!)

About twenty of us made up what became known as the Cahill Gang (because we had wiener roasts in Mr. Cahill's pasture). The core group changed little over the years, but new people came in, and some left, as they found other interests. While we were having loads of fun, we were still faithful to our churches. Many of us attended the then new Mt. Calvary Baptist Church in Albertville. Often our fun activities were church related, like picnics, singings, and revivals.

Several of us in the Cahill Gang were saved during a revival held in the Albertville Courthouse in 1938, before the Mt. Calvary Baptist Church was built. My own conversion came at that time. There were so many young people making decisions during the revival that some of the older people felt we were just playing "Follow the Leader," and our professions of faith just weren't real. The years have proved them wrong. Most of us have remained true and are serving the Lord today. My own conversion experience *then* is more real to me today than when it happened nearly sixty years ago when I was fourteen. I knew then God would use me in some special way as I surrendered my life to him. I never doubted that revelation.

During that heightened excitement of my mid-teen years, the week after I became a Christian, I met Cornelius Bright.

We were on a school bus going to Nashville to the Grand Ole
Opry. He was eighteen, and I was *nearly* fifteen. Back then,
folks in my hometown loved country music. (They still do!)
Going to Nashville, 125 miles away, to the Grand Ole Opry was
something we all did if we could scrape together eight dollars
for the trip. That eight dollars paid for transportation, lodging,
and a ticket to the show. Meals were extra.

While all ages filled the bus, I soon became aware of the
boys. We all teased back and forth, having a grand time, as the
trip progressed. I noticed the boy I liked best liked my friend.
She was flirtatious and outgoing, but I was shy. I decided not
to "fight" for his attention. She could have him!

Unknown to me, of course, Cornelius was in his bachelor
mode at that time. He purposely rejected the attraction he felt
toward me. But when I pretended I didn't care and paid attention to the other boys, he decided I'd probably be worth getting
to know. That trip started a courtship of four years. During
those maturing years we both dated other people. Some of our
friends thought this was a danger to our relationship, but
Cornelius and I always knew we were meant for each other,
and that someday we'd be married.

CHAPTER 2

God of the Foxhole Experience

QUITE EARLY IN HIS LIFE CORNELIUS DECIDED HE WOULD not be a farmer. Once he was so angry and frustrated when he had to pick up cornstalks that he stood on a stump and shouted for all to hear, "I'll tell you one thing. If I ever get married and have any kids they won't have to pick up cornstalks!"

In 1939 Cornelius went to Florida to seek his fortune. Actually he went to work on a dairy farm. After a few months he decided that was too much like farming. So, in 1940 he joined the navy. I missed him, but I was proud of him, too. He took basic training at Norfolk, Virginia, and Aviation Machinist School at Jacksonville, Florida. Finally he was assigned to the Corpus Christi, Texas, Naval Air Station.

I had been happy to attend Snead Junior College in Boaz, Alabama, while Cornelius was in training, but once he was assigned to a base, we started making wedding plans. Cornelius had leave coming up in June, so we planned the wedding for June 14, 1942. The church, Mt. Calvary Baptist in Albertville, the preacher, Reverend D. E. Latham, and the attendants were all ready and waiting. But Uncle Sam wouldn't cooperate! Cornelius's leave was cancelled due to the worsening of the war.

Cornelius Bright in Corpus Christi, Texas, 1942.

Didn't the United States government know you never inter-fere with a bride's wedding plans? I went to Texas, not about to let a global war keep me from marrying my sweetheart. Cornelius had said, "Honey, whatever you do, don't come on July 4th, for I have the duty and can't meet your bus."

At that time I didn't know or care about navy rules and regu-lations. I just knew I was in love and wanted to get married. So, what did I do? I arrived in Corpus Christi on Saturday night, July 4, at 9:00 P.M. Of course I'd let Cornelius know my arrival time. For a minute, the surging sea of sailors at the bus station made me wonder if I'd been wise to come on July 4. Then, suddenly, I saw Cornelius. He'd met my bus after all! Some time later I learned all he'd gone through to meet my bus. I was most grateful to his Officer of the Day for making an exception and letting Cornelius "swap" duty with another sailor that night.

We were married on Monday, July 6, 1942, in the home of Reverend R. O. Cawker, pastor of First Baptist Church. Our best man, Rudy Ortiz, was as nervous as we were, but Pastor

Cawker, who had performed countless wedding ceremonies for sailors and their sweethearts, spoke so warmly of marriage being ordained of God and blessed by him, we soon settled down to enjoy the ceremony.

It's no wonder the First Baptist Church came to mean so much to us. We especially enjoyed the Young Marrieds Sunday School Department. Cornelius had been saved when he was nine years old—almost at his father's knee—but he had not been baptized. Ann Wollerman, the Church Educational Director, led him to see the need, and he was baptized. (Ann later became a missionary to Brazil, and she remained an inspiration to us.)

It was also at First Baptist that Cornelius became convinced that tithing was not only taught in the Scriptures but was necessary if one wanted to be obedient to Christ (Matt. 23:23). I had been tithing since I became a Christian and had taken for granted that Cornelius had, too. But he hadn't. It was a new revelation to him. What a happy time that was for us, to see and feel God's sure, gentle guidance taking effect in our lives.

During those wonderful months in Corpus Christi, we made several lifelong friends. Among them were the William Russell family and Clyde and Eleanor Chally. Though Mr. and Mrs. Russell have long since died, Ruth, their daughter, remains a steadfast friend. Clyde and Eleanor Chally were special to Cornelius and me because we slipped off with them to San Antonio, to stand up with them as best man and matron of honor. They had to marry secretly because she was in nurse's training and he was in flight school. They were not allowed to get married while in training.

A special treat for Ruth Russell and me was to be able to attend Clyde and Eleanor's fiftieth wedding anniversary party a few years ago in Austin, Texas.

Cornelius and my contented togetherness in Corpus Christi was interrupted when Cornelius received orders to go overseas—to the South Pacific. I returned to Alabama. I had completed two years at Snead Junior College, so I went on to the University of Alabama to finish my degree in education.

I wrote Cornelius every day, and he wrote me almost every day. At times the mail wouldn't get through either way, and we'd be miserable until we heard from each other. Sometimes I'd get a dozen letters at one time. And I treasured every one of them. Even though I was having a good time in my classes and doing my practice teaching, I still missed Cornelius terribly.

To help fill the empty hours, I became a Girls Auxiliary (G.A.) leader for Calvary Baptist Church—the campus church. I had not been a G.A. member as a girl, but I loved missions and was willing to learn. Actually the girls and I learned together. Helping them learn their "Forward Steps" taught me to memorize much Scripture, just as the girls had to. The mission studies and activities we did excited me.

Cornelius was not having a good time. Enemy planes attacking the base every night was not enjoyable. During those dangerous raids, when protecting our naval planes on

Foxhole on Morati Island
(Molucca Islands between
Indonesia and New Guinea).

the ground was paramount, Cornelius realized death was only a breath away. Seeing buddies fall in battle when their planes didn't return after going out to hit a target made Cornelius think very seriously about his own life.

One particularly difficult night raid sent Cornelius and all the ground crews to the foxholes. It was then and there, on a lonely island in the South Pacific, that Cornelius Bright surrendered his life to serve God wherever he wanted. He was already a Christian, but this commitment was to make Christ Lord of his life. That was one foxhole experience that was lived out when the serviceman returned home.

When Cornelius returned to the States in December 1945, I went to California to be with him. And, yes, he met my train! We settled into navy life (he had one year to go on a six-year hitch) in Alameda, California. What a growing year that was for us. We worked with Pastor E. K. and Holly Dougherty in the First Southern Baptist Church of Alameda. It was later named Central Baptist for the street on which the church was built.

We were challenged by Brother Dougherty's vision for starting missions to grow churches. Equally challenging was Mrs. Dougherty's absolute trust and confidence in us. The two Doughertys took us, and all the other servicemen and their families, and led us to serve the Lord. This was in 1946, and the Lord seemed to be saying to us, "You, Cornelius and Edna Bright, learn all you can right here, for this foretells your future." What a nurturing church that was!

By now we had been married nearly four years, and we were anxious to start our family. My problem-free pregnancy ended in a fifty-four hour labor that gave us Princess Alona, on November 4, 1946. She was born in the Oakknoll Naval Hospital in Oakland, California. She immediately filled our hearts with joy, and fear, adding a whole new dimension to our lives.

We reveled in caring for Alona and made the normal mistakes, but we assured each other we could handle that seven pounder—in time. The long hard delivery left Princess

Alona with a nervous stomach. The Kaeopectate the doctor prescribed returned to us more often than it stayed with her. Before long, though, she must have realized we'd keep spooning it in, for she finally kept it down and became a very good baby.

That eventful year—1946—passed all too quickly. Cornelius mustered out of the navy in December, and we headed east in January 1947. Princess Alona was two months old. Our first car, a 1935 Ford, had no heater in it, but that didn't faze us, for we were headed home. Brother Dougherty cautioned us to take the southern route to avoid the ice and snow. We took the southern route all right, but in Tombstone, Arizona, we were told by the highway patrol to get off the road and find a motel. The roads were becoming impassable. We were snowbound!

Imagine our consternation when we finally found a motel room, but it had no heat. We reloaded the Ford and started out again, even as the blizzard continued. I think we feared we might freeze to death in that unheated motel room. We

The 1935 Ford that brought us safely home, 1946.

ventured on for another seventy-five miles and finally found a motel with heat.

I look back on that experience and am amazed that we made it. Princess Alona was the least of our worries. She was breastfed, and we had plenty of diapers and blankets to keep her warm. The '35 Ford was another matter. We must have prayed it through every mile. We believed driving on through the blizzard—sometimes not able to see the road—was the right thing to do. We were calm, believing God would take care of us. What confidence we had in him.

Eventually we made it to Dallas and then to the home of our Corpus Christi friends, the Russells. They had just survived a grasshopper siege that fall. Every tree and shrub was stripped of foliage. The countryside was barren. And the Russells were having "water problems" when we arrived. But you'd never guess it. They welcomed us with open arms of love and warmth and joy, especially in seeing Princess Alona.

Four days later we resumed our eastward journey. That little old Ford and that two-and-a-half-month-old baby, as well as her parents, welcomed the more moderate weather as we traveled southeastward. We made it to Alabama just fine. Our parents were overjoyed to see us well and healthy. They'd worried about us, especially about our "reckless endangerment" of setting out from California with a new baby in an eleven-year-old car with no heater. Grandparents are prone to feel that way when it concerns their grandchildren. Especially a new one.

After extended visits with both families, we were ready to get on with our plans. Cornelius, eager to get into college and prepare for whatever God wanted him to do, enrolled in Howard College (now Samford University) in Birmingham. It was hard for him. He had quit school to go to Florida and then to join the navy. That was a definite hindrance to him. He was academically unprepared for college level work. He tried to work (the G.I. Bill just didn't cover expenses) and go to school full time.

Cornelius had a responsible job as maintenance supervisor at Yielding Brothers Department Store, but his schoolwork suffered. At last he saw he would have to drop out of school for a while to support our family. We had grown to four when June Marie was born on February 16, 1949, at the East End Hospital in East Lake.

We were a busy, happy family. When June Marie was two and a half years old, we put the girls in daycare, and I began teaching. Cornelius was able to return to school full time. He graduated in 1958 with the first class on the new campus. We always joked about it taking him eleven years to finish a four-year course. I admired Cornelius for sticking with it and graduating.

Our Birmingham years were spent in Lake Highland and Fourth Avenue Baptist Churches. We grew by leaps and bounds by helping Fourth Avenue—a new church—get on its feet and start growing. Guthrie and Jane Curtis and Knox and Ruth Johnston, the two pastors while we were there, were always supportive of our "call" to pioneer missions. Fourth Avenue

Our first pastor family at Fourth Avenue Baptist Church in Birmingham, Jane and Guthrie Curtis and sons.

Knox and Ruth Johnston, pastor at Fourth Avenue Baptist Church when we left Birmingham. Cornelius (center) carries the proverbial hobo's bag, and Alona and June, our daughters, are seated at left bottom.

Baptist Church gave much money through the years to help support the churches we started.

More and more we felt drawn to starting churches. Living in the deep South, in the comfort zone of many churches, Baptist and otherwise, dulls one to the evangelistic needs in the rest of the country. We knew our call was to help meet those needs in new areas where churches were few and far between and Baptist churches almost nil.

Cornelius's graduation behind us now, we headed for the seminary in Fort Worth, Texas. I taught school the first year at John T. White and the second year at Carter Park Elementary. Cornelius was able to attend seminary full time. Alona and June attended school where I taught until Alona reach junior high. Then she attended Rosemont Junior High School. We attended the Eighth Avenue Baptist Church. Cornelius and I worked in the Young Marrieds Sunday School Department where we made some lasting friendships. It was there we met

Don and Lorene Salyer who became very important to us later in Warren, Ohio.

By now, we were sure God wanted us in pioneer missions. With that conviction, Cornelius went to Ohio as a summer missionary in 1959. He partnered with John Ross, another student summer worker. Together they worked ten weeks in the northwestern corner of Ohio where Southern Baptist churches were young and small, but growing. Their main jobs were knocking on doors doing survey and witnessing, helping in Vacation Bible Schools (VBS), leading song services, and "preaching" in revival services. It was a memorable summer for Cornelius. He came home convinced of what the "anything" he promised God in the foxhole would be. We had complete peace about the call to help start churches.

That summer while Cornelius was gone, I attended the seminary. My classes challenged and thrilled me. My favorite was Missions 101 with Dr. Cal Guy. He was a great teacher. He certainly made missions come alive. There's no doubt that summer deepened our understanding and commitment to serve the Lord.

It was a growing summer for Alona and June, too. Now approaching thirteen, Alona was mature and independent. She loved the piano and played for hours. She became the boss of the house when I was in classes.

June spent the summer enjoying the freedom of being unfettered. She and the neighborhood boys and girls played ball, built forts, teased their pets, and played in the local cray-fish hole. She seemed deliriously happy.

Our summer arrangement had one serious drawback. Sometimes Alona, as boss, refused to let June in the house because she "smelled so awful." June's playing with the pets, as well as catching crayfish, tended to make Alona's accusations believable. However, even a smelly sister deserved bathroom privileges.

Because we were now committed to starting churches, we applied to the Home Mission Board's Tentmaker Program. This program, then under the direction of Dr. Fred McCauley, was an effort to get Southern Baptists to move into pioneer areas, provide their own livelihood, and help start churches.

We asked to be assigned to Alaska or Hawaii because we had friends in those faraway places: Bill and Margaret Hansen in Alaska and Joe and Blanche Morgan in Hawaii. Of course, we assured the Home Mission Board staff we were ready and willing to go wherever we were needed.

About this time, right before seminary graduation, Cornelius was offered a position as educational director for a large, well-established church in Michigan. It would have been a wonderful opportunity for him to use his spiritual gifts and the people skills he'd honed in seminary. It would have been good, too, for us, as a family, to no longer have to struggle financially. But we didn't even consider it. For us it would not have been right. Our hearts were turned to starting churches. At that point, I doubt we could have done anything else.

Upon graduation, the Home Mission Board asked us to go to Warren, Ohio. That was a far cry from Alaska or Hawaii, but it was most surely where God wanted us. In a leap of faith we took everything we owned—our daughters, our furniture, and our 1953 Chevrolet—to a city we'd never seen before, to start Southern Baptist work, to grow a church. We were so happy.

We knew no one in Warren, Ohio, but Paul Nevels, Cuyahoga Baptist Associational Missionary from Cleveland, had a family for us to meet. Wilfred and Lelia Roden, and year-old son Albert, lived in Niles, about ten miles from Warren. Lelia was a Southern Baptist who grew up in New Mexico and Wilfred, a native son of Ohio, was raised American (Northern) Baptist.

The Rodens welcomed the four of us with true Christian hospitality. They were our lifesavers then and have remained extra-special friends through the years. They added Hallie, Pam, and Neal to their family and have meant much to several churches started in that corner of Ohio.

Within two weeks, Cornelius and I had teaching positions, he and Paul Nevels found a place for the non-existent church to meet, and, with no money, we'd bought a house and moved into it. Those miracles confirmed that God was in control, and he was making a way for us to serve him.

That was truly a humbling time. It assured our hearts that when God's people step out on faith to do what he has called them to do, he will provide for them. That truth was demonstrated over and over again through the years as we encouraged young pastors to "come north." No, the way is not always clear, nor the provisions at hand, but when one steps out on faith to do his will, God makes things happen.

CHAPTER 3

Earning the Right to Be Heard

LEARNING AT THE FEET OF GREAT TEACHERS WAS exciting to Cornelius. This had been especially true of seminary professors. Their humility, despite outstanding scholarship, inspired him. So, he learned a great lesson when one of his professors at Southwestern told the class one day, "If you really want to win people to Christ, first, share the gospel and then put on a demonstration of the difference the gospel makes in your life. That's how you earn the right to be heard."

When Cornelius and I went for job interviews with the Warren Board of Education, the members were surprised that we were white. I asked them why. They said they had expected us to be black because of our accent (on the phone) and because we were from Alabama. They were impressed enough to hire me immediately for the city schools, and Cornelius took a position in the Southington Schools, just outside of Warren.

The shock of their assumption was an eye-opener for us. It felt strange—most uncomfortable—to be on the receiving end of prejudicial attitudes. Even among my teacher friends, my accent was amusing. They'd ask me to repeat, or say things, for their enjoyment. We often played the "I will, if you will" game.

For each time they asked me to say words like "oil," I'd ask them to say "creek." Mostly it was fun. Alona and June faced the same kind of teasing, but we were all soon assimilated into the school systems.

I was honestly surprised and amazed at the erroneous perceptions they held of the South and southern people. Once, my gracious principal, Vivian Vera Viets, made a lasting impression on me and taught me a great lesson at that same time. It was in March 1962. Cornelius and I lost his mother and my father in the same week. While we were home, Miss Viets called. She asked if there was anything at all they could do for us. I assured her we were fine, that I appreciated her call, and that we'd be back in Warren by the weekend.

Later, back in Warren, I thanked Miss Viets again for her call. She said, "Well, the teachers and I were so worried because it was so cold, and the houses in the South are less substantially built than they are here; we just thought we might need to help in paying heating and other bills."

Their ignorance floored me. I asked where she got her information on houses in the South. I knew she had never been south. Now, here were college-trained teachers and their principal making judgments on something they knew nothing about. They believed the tales equally ignorant writers wrote, willing to put down anything southern. They especially loved repeating all the negative things about race relations in the South.

I made it a point to admit we did have problems in the South, but looking around Warren, I saw some of the same problems and even some we didn't have. I tried to be kind, because prejudices exist in every section of the country, but I wanted them to know they had been misguided. I challenged them, "Go south and see for yourself. That's what I've done in coming north."

Since we knew why we were in Warren, we didn't let side distractions become important to us. Cornelius had learned much about people in the navy. He had friends of nearly every ethnic group and religious persuasion. But now we were to minister in a new way for us. We lived in a community that knew nothing about us, who associated Southern Baptists with "Holy

Rollers"—generally ignorant, uncultured southern people. Living in what they considered the culturally advantaged "north," they considered people in the South to be poorly educated and disadvantaged.

They soon learned better. In the seven years I taught in Warren, I worked with educators throughout the city. Attitudes changed and mutual respect resulted from my teaching and serving on school committees. The people in Warren had seen many "fly-by-night" church starts. They supposed ours would be the same. When it wasn't, they took notice. Remember! Share the gospel, put on a demonstration . . .

One of my friends at school, the kindergarten teacher, joined our church and became our choir director. Eugenia was engaged to be married in July 1961. She asked Cornelius to perform the wedding ceremony, but he had not been ordained. Since the state of Indiana, where the wedding would be held, required ministers to be ordained, Cornelius

Eugenia Harney and Arthur Lutes in front of Austin Village Baptist Church (shopping center).

acquiesced, in this instance, and was ordained on June 28, 1961. All of the Brights went to Ellwood, Indiana, for the wedding of Eugenia Harney to Arthur Lewellen Lutes. It was very special for all of us and a milestone for Cornelius. Many weddings followed, so it was good to have that requirement satisfied.

As a teacher representative at the monthly superintendent's meeting, I was able to voice concerns about things I believed the schools should be aware of. For instance, I objected to PTA meetings (mandatory teacher attendance) being held on Wednesday nights. I was told that prayer meeting was mostly unheard of, so it couldn't be important. So much for the tradition so ingrained in Southern Baptists! I also objected to school programs being held on Sunday mornings (requiring pupil attendance). Again I was the odd ball. They didn't see it as a problem.

I objected strenuously to the school policy that required teachers to avoid having biblical plays/ programs at Christmas. I thought that rule was ludicrous, so I broke it. And yes, I got into trouble for doing so. When I refused to change to a secular play, my principal told me to take it up with the superintendent. (Remember, this was in the early 1960s.)

I took a copy of the play to the superintendent and explained how the class had chosen it. We'd read several plays, secular and religious, but, by class vote, had chosen that particular play. My meeting with the superintendent was amicable. I left the play with him. The next morning he called me at school and told me to go ahead with the play.

I didn't always win. I was told, sometimes forcefully, that teachers were not to get involved with their students' out-of-school lives. But as a Christian, I knew I had to be involved.

Cornelius enjoyed teaching at Southington and was well liked by the teachers and pupils. He was approached about becoming principal of the elementary school. He assured them he could not consider it. His commitment to grow a Southern Baptist church was his goal. After two years, he quit teaching and devoted full time to the church.

Alona and June were enrolled in Warren G. Harding High School and Turner Junior High respectively. Both were good students. Alona loved A Cappella Choir more than her other studies. June was into cheerleading and playing the flute. We suspected her desire to play the flute was so she could play and march with the band at school events.

Both girls were invaluable help in getting the Austin Village Baptist Church in Warren started. We may have overused them by insisting they always be there. They made friends easily and helped develop our young people's groups. A special blessing to the church was their ability to play the piano.

Many beginning churches are hindered in their worship experiences because they lack good pianists, so we were blessed. Alona and June sang well, too, and often contributed to our worship services. Neither Cornelius nor I was musically adequate, but having the girls—both talented—was a tremendous help. Some of my fondest memories of those early years have to do with their enrichment of our programs.

Have you ever noticed how some people ignore the built-in hardships a pastor's family lifestyle is for the children? It is especially hard for teenagers. That is true even in the well-churched areas of the South. It is doubly true in new work areas because the pastor's family becomes role models for the church members and for the community they are trying to reach.

I know there were times when Alona and June just did not want to go to church. They wanted a break just to not go. But, right or wrong, from the parenting standpoint, Cornelius and I felt it was necessary for them to be faithful in attendance. Just to stay home, or to go elsewhere, was not acceptable to us. Alona sometimes wanted to go to church with her friends, at the same time we were having services. We frowned on that, a fact she resented. It's possible we overdid that aspect of their upbringing.

One job Alona and June never liked, but did to help me, was contacting the nursery workers for the extended services.

The church policy was to ask adult volunteers to stay once a month with children under four years old. I'd make a three-month roster (schedule) of the volunteers and post it. During the week of their time to serve, I'd call and remind them. Because of my over-crammed schedule, I couldn't get the calling done sometimes. That's when the girls would do it for me. Their complaints were few and far between, but I knew it wasn't their favorite thing. I considered it a ministry, myself, and tried to get the girls to see it that way. I don't think I succeeded.

A family affair. That's how we always looked at our serving the Lord. Alona and June had become Christians when they were young, nine and seven, at Fourth Avenue Baptist Church in Birmingham. We knew, as parents, that we set the emotional and spiritual tone of our home and our service to the Lord. We included Alona and June in family decisions. We initiated what we called family council time. It was not held on a schedule, but just when things came up that needed everyone's input before a decision was made. Sometimes those meetings were fun, even hilarious. At other times they were serious and thought provoking.

The ground rules for the family council were few and simple: 1) Begin with prayer; 2) Each person freely express his/her thoughts; 3) Criticize as much as you want—in love; and 4) End with prayer. It can be a startling revelation for a parent to, unforeseen, hear a child speak words of anger and frustration about a situation the parent had long since forgot. It can be a thrill to have your child compliment you when you thought no one noticed or cared you'd made special effort on something. I highly recommend the family council to young families, provided they don't hold their children's words against them. It can help parents understand their children, and it can show the children that Mom and Dad are fair and willing to listen.

When we first started the church in Warren, Ohio, God provided our space. Cornelius and Paul Nevels (area missionary out of Cleveland) found a vacant unit in the Austin

Paul and Daisy Nevels, with daughter, April. Paul was our area missionary.

Village Shopping Center in Warren. They checked it out and felt it was the place we needed. They knelt in the office of that unit and prayed for the future church.

Later that week, they met with the shopping center manager. They asked him if we could rent that unit for the church. Mr. Harris explained, "We rent that unit for three hundred dollars a month." It did have nice carpet, an office, and a full, usable basement. But for a church with no members, three hundred dollars a month was pretty steep, especially in 1960.

Paul Nevels said, "This is a new, just beginning church. They can pay only one hundred dollars a month."

Mr. Harris shook his head and said, "I'll take your offer to the owners, but I'm sure they won't accept it. You'd better keep looking for a place."

The following Monday, Mr. Harris told Cornelius we could have the unit for one hundred dollars a month, provided we'd vacate it immediately, should they find another renter. We gladly agreed.

Austin Village Baptist Church began on July 10, 1960. In attendance that first Sunday were Cornelius and I, Alona, June, and two summer missionaries, Sally Lippy and Nancy Brown. That "auspicious" beginning was followed by a Vacation Bible School—sixteen enrolled—and a revival the next week with a high attendance of thirty-three.

Thus began a very good relationship with the Austin Village Shopping Center management. As the church grew, we needed more space. We asked for another unit in the shopping center. We were given one, four doors up the street, for no extra rent. It became our preschool and children's building. The youth used the basement of the first unit, and the adults met in the carpeted worship area.

In no way am I saying those were ideal quarters for beginning a new church, for they weren't. We had a corner A&P Grocery Store on our left. Separating the two units on the right were a beverage store, a state liquor store, and a piano store. But you must remember this: God never told us to find a perfect, sanctified place to start a church. He, himself, sanctified the premises as we met to worship, praise, honor, and exalt him.

One Sunday, early Sunday School arrivals found two feet of water in the basement. Ken McVickers, our fearless Sunday School director, in his Sunday best, pulled on Cornelius's waders and carefully retrieved our youth teaching materials. Then he searched for and found the plug for the drain. He pulled it, and all the water rushed out. Everything was back to normal the next Sunday.

We started a full church program at Austin Village with Sunday School, Church Training (then), and the mission groups we had leadership for. We longed for the people to love and understand Acts 1:8 and Matthew 28:19–20, so we always started Baptist Women, Royal Ambassadors (R.A.), and G.A.s. As soon as we could get leadership trained, we began Young Women's Auxiliary, Mission Friends, and Brotherhood. I'm sure you can guess who the leaders were in the beginning. Of course such a program was demanding and exhausting. It was such a boon to us personally, and to the church, when other leaders either moved into our community, joined the church, and accepted leadership roles, or we "grew our own." The latter takes more time!

In spite of the negatives about the church's location, people continued to visit our services. And, as the Lord led, many joined the church. With a Home Mission Board loan we bought property on Commerce Street, two blocks behind the shopping center. It was a rapidly growing residential area. We could hardly wait to build a house of worship!

Timing is so important in starting new churches. It helps to insure continuing growth. The timing was just right for two great boosts to our work in northeastern Ohio. They came in Don Salyer, a pharmacist from Texas, who came as our unpaid educational director, and Ross Hughes, who came as the first director of missions for the Steel Valley Baptist Association.

Don and Lorene Salyer, with daughter Kim and son Glen, whom we had known in Fort Worth, moved to Warren in 1963. Lorene taught school, and Don was pharmacist at Warren General Hospital. They had a third child, Rodney, while in Warren. Don and Lorene were trained church workers who had been Foreign Mission volunteers. Their expertise and dedication eased our personal leadership roles tremendously. It was so wonderful to have someone who understood our dreams and goals for the Lord's work. Don led our Sunday School to be standard and better!

In 1965, Ross and Pauline Hughes moved to Warren. From day one they proved to be just what the churches needed. Ross, with his ever present "Where the People Are" charts, helped us in starting new work and strengthening the churches we had. Ross Hughes believed and published that Ohio—Steel Valley in particular—was a good place to invest one's life for Christ.

Pauline Hughes was the epitome of love and Christian graciousness. She was an excellent teacher and visitor. Her kind, helpful spirit permeated all she did, making it a joy to be in her presence. As time passed, Ross and Pauline became favorites with all the churches in the association.

Never bothered by small numbers, Ross put this note in his associational mail-out, in the "Where But In Ohio" column:

Three records of 17 on October 24th. Boardman, Masury, and New Castle each had 17 in services October 24th. This was a record in each place so far. All three began last summer.

Maybe you had to be living and working in missions in Ohio in the 1960s to appreciate that newsworthy item. The great heart and dedication to serve the Lord and his people never failed where Ross and Pauline Hughes were concerned.

In one of his mail-outs, Ross quoted Dr. Jeff D. Ray, long-time professor at Southern Seminary, saying, "Brethren, always be kind to everybody because everybody is having a HARD TIME."

Ross Hughes added his own thoughts to that quote:

Rejoice with every Christian living in the will of God for that one is having a wonderful time. Of course it's HARD. The most attractive LIE of the Devil is that one about soft, problemless living being a WONDERFUL LIFE. Men and women, finding God's wonderful solutions to hard problems, find the most exciting, alive, inspired, joyful, blessed living in this world.

Pioneer Mission problems are many and multiple. To see God at work answering prayers and giving beyond that which is asked or thought is WONDERFUL LIVING. God is every-where and says in Jeremiah 33:3, "Call unto me and I will answer thee, and show thee great and mighty things, which thou knowest not."

At Austin Village, we were so eager to get into our new building we scheduled a baptismal service before it was finished. We'd grown weary of having to find a place to baptize. Sometimes we'd use the Christian Church's baptistry or an outside pond. We longed for our own baptistry for ourselves and our missions, since we were all growing. For months, after ours was installed, we, or one of our missions, baptized every fourth Sunday. Sometimes there were over a dozen candidates.

On this particular Sunday morning, Cornelius got to the church early, as was his custom. But this morning he came to check the newly installed baptistry, to see if it had filled properly. To his dismay, he found the baptistry steps floating on top of the water. He rushed to the phone to tell me to bring him extra underwear. He asked Don Salyer to stand guard while he stripped to his shorts, plunged into the baptistry, and anchored the steps.

As people arrived that morning, Don directed them to the kitchen, the office, the nursery—anywhere away from the auditorium. But others, whom Don didn't intercept, marched directly into the auditorium just as Cornelius finished dressing in the side room. He came out all smiles as if nothing was amiss. Later we laughed about the pastor being the first one immersed in our new baptistry.

Austin Village dedicated its building on July 11, 1965, five short years after the first service in the shopping center. William Slagle, area missionary, preached in the morning service. Paul Nevels, former missionary, preached the dedicatory sermon in the afternoon. We were full of gratitude for the Home Mission Board's loans and support, as well as that of so many others. It was a moving experience for the whole congregation. We acknowledged that God had grown a church in a dry and thirsty land. The Austin Village Baptist Church stood as a testimony to God's grace and his faithfulness. We stood in awe of what he had accomplished.

In 1962, we'd started a mission at Newton Falls, west of Warren. No, we didn't wait until everything was perfect at Austin Village before we reached out to another community. A small cluster of southerners, who had come north to work during World War II and stayed, were eager to have a church started near them. Raymond and Irene Franklin came as pastor, and that church was on its way. Their fine children added much to their efforts, just as ours had done at Austin Village. In fact, we found it consistently true that the children of our mission pastors were always a plus. They seemed happy to make church planting a family affair.

Next we started Central Baptist Church, south of Warren in Niles. Charles and Dorothy Brashear came as pastor in 1964. That year we began the work in Youngstown that became known as Austintown Baptist Church. Ron and Evelyn Martin, from Oklahoma, came to pastor that mission. In 1966, Churchill/Liberty Church was started in Girard. Tom and Joyce Theriot served there.

If I could tell you the birth pains and struggle to survive, experienced by every mission we started, you would not believe it. I can't do that, but I can tell you the key to their survival was prayer that went into their beginnings, and the pastoral leadership that came because God called them. When these and other churches were started, it was our hope, and theirs, that they would be instrumental in starting other churches, that, in turn, would start still other churches. They faithfully did that. That's why we always spoke of children and grandchildren of the Austin Village Baptist Church in Warren. And the thrill was that there was always "another on the way."

When we left Warren in 1967, there were thirteen churches that had been started by Austin Village and her missions. On returning for their twentieth anniversary, we heard Don Davidson, director of missions, say, "Austin Village has ten children, thirty grandchildren, and three great-grandchildren." And the work goes on.

When speaking of husband and wife coming to a church as pastor, I hope I'm not offending anyone. I consider it biblical because Jesus speaks of marriage making us one. But, of course, my meaning is that a man, even a man of God, (however good he may be alone) is completed with a loving, supportive wife. This is not to say every pastor has to be married because God calls some men (and women) to remain single. But God brings a man and a woman together in love that they may serve him with one heart and one dedication.

I always felt a part of the decision-making process in our family. When Cornelius was approached about a new job, a new place of service, or opportunity, I was informed about it. We made decisions together. I couldn't conceive of him making such decisions without me, without praying with me about them. Quite honestly, my only concern was that we be in God's will. The where and how could always be worked out if we felt it was what God wanted.

We always prayed with the girls, too, before making important decisions. We valued their concerns. Since Cornelius and I were educators, we thought we knew our girls. But, the truth is, none of us ever truly knows another person, not even our own children. Believing that to be true, I asked Alona and June to write a memory (one or more) of the years they were growing up when we were church planters.

Because I trust them completely, I promised I'd include any memory they wrote, good or bad, flattering or otherwise. Their memories follow. Alona's is first, not because she is the older of the two, but because what she said speaks volumes on how children in a preacher's family sometimes feel. June's, on the other hand, leads naturally into the next chapter in this book.

ALONA'S MEMORIES

Spending my teenage years on a mission field in "Yankee Land," as the Alabama relatives dubbed Ohio, was both an exciting adventure and a lonely passage. The people I came to know there, as well as those who visited us, and school and church music were the nourishing aspects of my life. However, loneliness was the overwhelming feeling I had in those years. I had few friends, no social life except church, and parents who were emotionally unavailable to me.

I was thirteen years old when our family pulled into a strange driveway in Niles, Ohio, and was robustly welcomed by the Roden family in whose home we were to stay until we could find our own place to live. We'd never met those folks, but they accepted us right away. It took about two weeks to find a house and a place for the church to begin meeting. During that time our two families formed a bond that has remained strong to this day.

In our new house, June and I had our own rooms upstairs! There was a room for Daddy to use as an office, and there was even a garage for the car! (We hadn't yet experienced an Ohio winter to know that garages were a necessity.) The church was to meet in a store unit of the neighborhood shopping center. And both Mom and Dad found teaching jobs for the school year. There were some miracles concerning all those transactions, though I don't recall the details. I do remember hearing Mother and Daddy talk about how God had provided everything we needed. It certainly built my faith.

Going to church at first seemed "odd." Often there were fewer than ten people at church, but we had Sunday School and a full worship service just as if there had been hundreds. Growth was steady as new people were reached, but for most of the six years, I was the only kid my age who came regularly. In a small congregation it was noticeable when Mother and June would giggle during church when they sat together. I never quite knew why they giggled. Maybe it was the singing or my piano playing. Daddy got sort of frustrated with them sometimes. (Actually, I think *mad* would be more like it!)

The whole reason for being in church was serious to Daddy. He was concerned about what others would think about us or how we might negatively influence those who saw us "acting up." He had a strong faith and spiritual eyes to see what was not yet visible. He wasn't a great speaker; in fact, he was very shy in the pulpit. But no one could ever doubt his love for people and his passion to see that each individual had an opportunity to respond to Jesus. Daddy was a pastor who modeled servanthood. He worked side by side with anyone who wanted to help build the church. He showed others how to live for Christ by his own life.

I remember several times when Daddy's love for people challenged our family routine. He occasionally brought home strangers he'd picked up somewhere. He'd let them shower and shave, gave them clean clothes, and expected Mother wouldn't mind when they joined us for a meal. Mother's frustration and Daddy's compassion created amusing tension around our dinner table more than once!

Mom and Dad had a shared call to ministry, and their partnership reflected that. Daddy was the dreamer, the visionary, the heart of the work. Mother was the pragmatist, the programmer, the one who made it happen. They worked together beautifully, encouraging each other's gifts. The fruit of their labors bears witness of how our gracious God uses ordinary folks to accomplish Kingdom purposes.

My school experiences in the North opened my eyes in many ways. Thoughts, ideas, and preconceived notions were challenged at every turn. Though we had been raised to treat all people with respect and dignity, it was in Ohio that I actually knew people of different races and religions. Prior to this, I had never attended school with black kids or Catholic kids or kids who never went to any church at all!

As a ninth grader, newly arrived from Texas with a fresh accent, I was teased constantly by boys in my homeroom class. They wanted to know where I hitched my horse, etc. It was good-natured fun and not hard to endure. I adjusted fairly well to the school routine.

In the tenth grade, at the consolidated high school where fewer people knew me, I was physically assaulted by two black girls who thought they heard me call them "niggers" across the softball field as we were coming in from P. E. I was too shocked to fight back as they pounded on me in the locker room. With my arms I tried to block the blows to my face and head. A teacher was summoned, and it was soon over. The physical bruising was minimal, but I was an emotional wreck for several days, nauseated by bewilderment about what had happened and why. I found out later that because I was a white person from the South the girls assumed I would hate them. They were wrong. I came to understand that because they were acting from incorrect information about me there was no need to get angry. I was somewhat insecure for a while, but within a few months one of the girls apologized to me, and we became friends.

Also, in tenth grade two grandparents died, and I got a "D" in geometry on my report card. I missed two weeks of school as the family shuttled back and forth to Alabama so Mom could be with her dad, and Daddy could be with his mother. They died within four days of each other. It must have been terribly difficult for them to be so far away from "home" when their hearts wanted to be there.

High school wasn't about academic scholarship for me. (June was our family representative in the National Honor Society.) Music was what kept me energized, feeling alive. As a member of a 120 voice nationally recognized A Cappella Choir, I was engrossed in all facets of that learning process. I loved rehearsing, memorizing, breathing practice, learning parts, keeping my voice on pitch, and listening to the magnificent sound when it all came together. The thrill of being a part of the music, in those rare moments, when every part merged perfectly, would carry me away into "glory"!

Piano was another part of my musical soul. I'd taken a smattering of lessons throughout my childhood, but the last few months before our move to Ohio I had a "crash course" in hymn playing, to prepare me to play for church. I did play, though not very confidently, for services from the beginning. The hymns moved beyond the keys of C, G, and F.

At church I sang solos occasionally, but it was hard. Daddy was fairly critical of my singing, saying, "If the people can't understand the words, you might as well not sing." But to help me he bought a very nice tape recorder/player to make it easier for me. I had to play the piano for myself and wasn't able to sing clearly from the piano with no microphone. The tape recorder enabled me to record the accompaniment at home, then sing with the tape at church.

Except for choir groups, summer missionaries, and friends and family who came to visit us, I didn't have much of a social life. I wanted to play sports after school, but getting me to and from events was too worrisome. Monday night choir practice was problematic enough. I attended two high school football games after I got my driver's license. I had one boyfriend at church and, later, one in choir at school, but I didn't date. I remember wanting to attend church with my friends and not being allowed to go because they met at the same time we did, and I couldn't miss our services. Finally, one night, I was allowed to go to a Thursday night revival service with my Church of the Nazarene friend.

My young life was rich with experiences and people, but I never felt I had the opportunity or the freedom to be myself. I often didn't feel supported in areas where I excelled. I don't recall my parents attending any of the concerts our choir gave because they were usually scheduled for Wednesdays—prayer meeting night. I had solos sometimes, but they weren't there. At church I was expected to act properly at *all* times, which included not chewing gum! I never felt quite good enough just being me.

I was not able to compete with God for my parents' attention. I seldom had any time with Daddy. He was either gone "visiting" or studying. Mother was around more, but always busy. The message I internalized was that I certainly wasn't as important as the church people who always had Daddy's focus, nor as the church programs that consumed Mother's time after she did housework and graded school papers. I was sometimes angry and resentful that they expected me to meet the expectations of *their* call to ministry. I felt like an accessory to the family who made myself useful by playing the piano for church. I don't remember having a family or a life outside the church. I missed a lot.

The character qualities that made Mom and Dad a great ministerial team were channeled through the funnel of their commitment to the high calling of God on their lives. I am grateful for the foundational precepts of God's Word my parents lived out before me. They were (and Mom continues to be) true to their call, faithful to their Lord. There was no deceit in their lives. They were who they appeared to be. When my heart breaks out of love for the people of God and the way we don't "do church" as Jesus taught us, I remind myself of Daddy. And when I want people to know the blessing of doing things right, of giving their hearts to the Lord, I sound like Mother. I'm not as concerned about what others may think of me as they were, but then I wasn't raised in the South! (Thank you, God!) I am proud of what my parents did and who they were. My life has been enriched because of the experiences I had tagging along with them.

CHAPTER 4

God Never Said It Would Be Easy

IT WAS IN NOVEMBER 1966, AT THE OHIO BAPTIST STATE Convention in Dayton, that Joe Waltz, director of missions for the Pittsburgh Baptist Association, and Frank Bowman, pastor of the South Park Baptist Church in Pittsburgh, approached Cornelius about going to Erie to start a Southern Baptist church. I could see and feel Cornelius's excitement as he told me about Erie County's two hundred thousand people without a Southern Baptist witness.

Our first response was to pray. And we did—long and hard. Wasn't God using us where we were? Shouldn't we stay and help the Steel Valley Association grow? We had our home there and had made so many good friends. . . .

In the end, we realized that God had already answered our prayers and our questions. Hadn't he sent Don and Lorene Salyer to help us at Austin Village? And weren't Ross and Pauline Hughes in place as associational missions director? The churches had dedicated pastors and were growing. As hard as it was to leave Warren, we knew it was time to move to a new field.

JUNE'S MEMORY
1960–1967

There are many memories of those years. Some (most) happy, some sad, some painful, some bittersweet, and some very sweet.

Perhaps I can recall and write about the transition that occurred in 1967. That was the year Daddy moved to Erie in February to begin the new work at Millcreek. He began going to Erie during the week while Mother and I stayed in Warren. He began networking with families there who were interested in starting a new church and looking for a place to meet. He would come back to Warren on Friday night or Saturday, and Mother and I would go with him to Erie for church services on Sunday. We'd all come back to Erie on Sunday night; then on Monday or Tuesday, Daddy would go back to Erie. That was the routine from February to June.

Alona was away at college, Mother was teaching and finishing the school year at Elm Road Elementary School, and I was finishing my senior year at Warren G. Harding High School. That was a happy year for me and one I appreciated then, and still do, for I had the opportunity to finish my school days there and maintain my connections with friends and activities. I knew it was a sacrifice for my parents to not be together, for my mother to carry on without my father, for Daddy to be on his own beginning the new work, and all the travel, etc.

Saying good-bye to Warren was hard. We'd lived there for nearly seven years. It was where my parents had established themselves in the work they wanted to do. Things had gone well, and the church was flourishing. I was proud of Daddy as the pastor of the church (a new church) when he gave the invocation at my graduation. It seemed we had come a long way from the humble beginning.

I remember the good-bye reception at the church on our last Sunday evening. Daddy and Mother were honored, and I was included in the festivities. At the end we were all asked to say a few words. I hadn't thought about this and hadn't prepared any words to say. Maybe it would have helped if I had, maybe not.

As I began to talk (I only said a few words and have no idea what they were), I became overwhelmed with emotion and began to cry. I tried to express my gratitude and depth of feeling for the people and place that were a *big* part of our lives. I knew I would miss everyone and the home community I felt I belonged to. I guess my tears expressed the thoughts and feelings I had.

Separations have always been difficult for me. It brought to mind then, as it does today, that the rest of my family seemed to accept and deal with these changes in ways that I did not. I'd known for some time that I was the one (still am) who expressed outwardly the emotions in the family—especially the sad ones. Somehow they always knew I would cry, and I did. No one ever seemed to mind or tell me not to.

I remember the truck had left with all our belongings. Daddy drove the truck and carried the two male summer missionaries with him. Alona drove one car and had the two female summer missionaries with her. Mother and I were to drive the other car. We were the last to leave. I recall going from one room of the house to the next, recalling memories and saying a last good-bye. I'm not sure what Mother was doing, perhaps saying good-bye in her own way, but I remember the feeling of a kindred spirit with her, as I knew she understood my sentiments.

Anyway, that move worked out as smoothly as anyone could imagine. We were moving to a lucky find of a house; we had four dear summer missionaries to move with us—helping to pack and then unpack and fill in time spaces open to loneliness. We had in them both company and help, and, as I realize now, we had four extra people to feed and find adequate living arrangements for. My parents somehow worked it out, and that summer was a very special one for all of us. I was preparing to go to college and was able to keep in touch with my high school friends by letter and a few visits over those three months.

I've always felt grateful for that time. I loved those years in Warren—they got better every year. I was sad to leave, but it came at a time I could bear it.

Alona and I left for college in September, she a senior and I a freshman. And Mother and Daddy began their "new" life in Erie, as a couple again.

Back to our move to Erie. I believe it's important to know that Frank Bowman had driven 150 miles weekly for a year to have Bible study with two families in Erie: the Ken Robinsons and the Glen Broddricks. Even before that, Charles Magruder had driven from Tonawanda, New York, to lead that same Bible study. Everyone thought it was time to have a man *on the field* in Erie. We told Pastor Bowman and the South Park Baptist Church we would go to Erie and, God willing, start a church.

Cornelius began cultivating Erie in February 1967, but June and I stayed in Warren to allow her to graduate with her class. Cornelius lived in the Glass Motel in Erie, and we joined him on weekends for the church services. This was a hard schedule to keep, but it did allow Cornelius to lay important groundwork for the new church.

In May 1967, Blanton Adair and six men from his church, Roebuck Plaza Baptist Church in Birmingham, went to Erie and did survey and visiting on behalf of the new church. Their being there created interest and excitement, and encouraged us.

We said our final good-byes to Warren, and with the help of our four summer workers (Ronnie Burkett, Rickey Jennings, Cindi Orr, and Karen Ower), moved to Erie on June 12, 1967. Cornelius had found a house we loved. We bought it—4641 Sterrettania Road—and it proved to be perfect for our ministry in Erie.

Less than a month after we moved, we celebrated our twenty-fifth wedding anniversary with a wonderful "open house." Many folks came from Warren and Pittsburgh and

Summer workers with Cornelius, standing in front of our house in Erie. Left to right: Rickey Jennings, Karen Ower, Cornelius, Cindi Orr, and Ronnie Burkett.

some from other cities. We even had several of our new Erie friends. Alona and June did all the planning and, with the help of their friends, all the work. At the risk of bragging, I must say we were so very proud of them.The day turned out to be one full of joy and memory making. As much as anything else, that celebration made us feel at home in Erie. We thanked God for our girls and for a new place to serve.

Church starting in Erie was different from that in Warren. For one thing, we had neither of our daughters with us. We missed their fun-loving ways and their abilities to help in a new church start.

Also, Erie was different in that we had two families to start with, the Robinsons and the Broddricks. However, Glen Broddrick got a job promotion that moved him to Chicago not long after we got to Erie. We knew that was a tremendous loss to the new work, but we were glad for his promotion.

Now we just had the Robinsons and the encouragement of our sponsoring church, South Park in Pittsburgh. But that was more than we had in Warren. We set out, convinced God wanted a church in Erie, and we wanted him to use us to bring it about.

We got permission to use the Millcreek Township Building for Sunday services, morning and evening, free of charge. All weekday activities: prayer meeting, planning sessions, mission organizations, and fellowships were held in our home. We had a full, finished basement which was adequate for large groups. As months and years passed, it proved to be a godsend.

We often used our home to house choir and mission groups who came to help us. On one occasion we had thirty-five people staying with us for survey and revival. Our evangelist, E. K. Dougherty, from California, slept on a half-bed in the office; a church member loaned us her new, never-used camper which slept four; and the rest of us slept in the upstairs bedrooms, the main floor living room and bedroom, and the more than ample basement. Admittedly, it was crowded, and

First members in Erie, Glen and Wanda Broddrick and sons.

the septic tank system rebelled, but the Lord worked through it all and saved souls that week.

Meals were fun, too. We'd take up the beds and set up the dining area in the basement. It worked like magic. Lest you think I did all the cooking for those groups, let me explain. The choir and mission groups came prepared with menus and cooks. They bought locally what they didn't bring with them for the meals. The young people were assigned days/meals when they were helpers for the adults in charge, either for cooking or for clean-up. I never saw their system fail. If the young people slacked off or tried to avoid their "turn," we never knew it. We were always pleased with the way the leaders worked with the young people. And the young people themselves were outstanding and a joy to have around.

Throughout the twenty-five years we were church planters, we often commented about the groups who came to help us being the normal, ordinary kind of kids and workers—just ordinary folks. But when they came to do God's work, the whole process took on a glow of his purpose and approval. They didn't come to please the Brights nor the Millcreek Church. They came to serve God and to tell people about his Son. We had genuine pride in all of them and were always grateful for the things they accomplished for the Lord and his church.

Another time, a choir group from Highlands Baptist Church in Ocala, Florida, stayed with us. That year, Larry Lewis, now former president of the Home Mission Board, was director of religious education for the Pennsylvania-South Jersey State Convention. He came to Erie and trained the Highlands Baptist Church young people how to do "door-to-door" witnessing. He also preached our revival that week. We had a tent set up for the services, but rain forced us indoors. The only *indoors* immediately available was a laundromat owned by one of our church members. I've often wondered if even God was amused by our improvisions. We, the congregation, sat among the washers and dryers; the choir stood in the more spacious entryway while they sang, then moved to the back of the laundromat. But Larry Lewis preached the Word in power, and God gave the increase! God can overcome our imperfections of space, if our hearts are bent on worshiping him.

What a challenge we had one year when we enrolled ninety-five in Vacation Bible School in our home. It was thrilling to see the learning groups in the three garages, the upstairs bedrooms, the living room, and, of course, the wonderful, spacious basement. The sheer magnitude of numbers caused our VBS workers to grow by leaps and bounds as they improvised daily, and, yet, shared the "old, old story of Jesus and his love." That year, my worker and I had seventeen three year olds. I remember it as a most joyous VBS. We learned a lot that year!

When our loan from the Home Mission Board came through, we were more than ready to start our building for the Millcreek Baptist Church. The Builders for Christ, out of Greenwood, Louisiana, were coming to construct it for us. We did the preliminaries, had the foundation slab poured, and the building materials on the site ready to go.

At their own expense, that wonderful group of people from Louisiana gave up vacation time to come help us build our building. Others from across the country got in touch with the Builders for Christ, or with us, and came to help. A special friend from seminary days, Bill Crews, our next door neighbor in Fort Worth, came. They began arriving on Saturday and were ready to start on the building early Monday morning.

How exciting it was to watch the building take shape under the direction of George Carkeet, their leader. He knew exactly what to do to keep things moving. We had prayer meeting in the open superstructure on Wednesday evening. By Saturday evening, the church building was housed in, and we had services in it Sunday morning. *The Erie Times*, our local paper, told the unbelievable story with pictures and an exceptionally positive article about the church. It was a great day indeed.

The finishing work was done by our men as they had time and opportunity. And it did take time. But on October 7, 1973, we dedicated the Millcreek Baptist Church to the glory of God and the salvation of man. We never ceased thanking God for the Builders for Christ and the others who came to help. They met our need for a building in a generous, loving way. How precious is the realization that God prompts his people to help fellow believers. Like Jesus, the Builders for Christ "went about doing good."

As mentioned before, starting churches in Erie was different from starting in Warren. I think the biggest reason was Erie was a closed community. The people felt they had all the churches they needed. The city was predominantly Catholic, and that influenced some things, but the closed attitude was evident in non-Catholics as well. And it was not just true of church-life, but other facets of life showed "closedness."

When you confront closed minds and hearts, you keep knocking on doors and visiting whoever welcomes you, but you must also find new ways to break the barriers. As a teacher, I gained permission to sponsor a public theatre showing of a great film, *Bill Wallace of China*. It was a dramatic, factual account of the way the Communists treated our missionaries, and other Americans, when they swarmed into China and took control of our Baptist Hospital there.

I was permitted to give tickets to anyone who would take them, but the only witnessing we could do was to have our church name and address on the tickets and advertising flyers. The three showings of the film brought only fair attendance— a total of 125 people. However, it did create some interest, and people who saw it mentioned it to us for months afterwards.

A most pleasurable thing we did, which was appreciated by the Millcreek Education Office, was to be one of the host families for Alba Gonzales, an exchange teacher from the Dominican Republic. Alba was Catholic and we offered to take her to any of the many Catholic churches in Erie, but she chose to attend our services while she was with us.

A haunting memory I have of Alba was when we took her to dinner at the Beachcomber—a delightful smorgasbord out on Presque Isle. It was a favorite spot for us to take our friends because they had an endless variety of excellent foods. Alba was overcome with all the choices. She burst into tears! We were surprised, to say the least. Upon regaining her composure, Alba explained, "I'm so sorry for these tears. I just can't see all this food without remembering how little my family has back in Santo Domingo. Please forgive me."

We assured Alba there was nothing to forgive. Personally, I never enjoyed the Beachcomber as much after that experience with Alba. We Americans have so much, we cease to be grateful for it. And just think, much of the world is starving!

A treat for Alba, while she was with us, was the experience of walking on water. Her home in Santo Domingo had a very warm climate, so snow and ice were novelties to her. She had never seen a lake frozen over. Presque Isle Bay, between Presque Isle and Erie City, often froze twenty to thirty inches deep, making it possible to walk out on the ice for several hundred yards quite safely. Some years the ice would be so thick cars would be driven out on it.

Alba very carefully started out and soon loved it! We took pictures of our antics, slipping and sliding, so she could prove to the folks back home that she really did "walk on water." However, Alba turned down Cornelius's invitation to go ice fishing—one of his favorite sports.

Some teaching Cornelius did outside the church walls, which garnered much respect and favorable response, was when he spoke, as a Baptist pastor, to classes at Mercyhurst College (a Catholic Girls' School). This opportunity came about by my having met the mother of one of my fifth graders. Erin told her mother I was a Baptist, married to a pastor, and that I knew a lot about the Bible. That stimulated the mother to ask me if Cornelius would come to Mercyhurst and teach her girls' classes what Baptists believe. The girls were studying different religions.

Cornelius enjoyed the classes and was at ease answering the girls' questions. He probably needed their questions as much as they needed his answers, for it helped him to know and understand their concerns. There were two main concepts they just couldn't grasp: 1) the priesthood of believers and

2) the autonomy of the local church. (I've known some Baptists who have trouble with those doctrines, too.)

When community gardens became popular again in Erie in the 1970s, Cornelius and I joined about forty other families, black and white, to use a donated hillside, just out of Erie City limits, to grow a "victory" garden. The victory for us was getting out in the community to enjoy people. Cornelius never wanted to be a farmer, but he loved the land in small portions. Hence, we always had a garden. We grew abundant crops and had plenty to share with friends and neighbors, as well as a lot to can and freeze.

I must admit, the physical work of the garden fell to Cornelius, but I enjoyed being outside with him and visiting with fellow gardeners. The black people planted the same kinds of crops we did, and it was fun to tease back and forth about the best way to cook okra, corn, squash, collards, and turnip greens. The other white gardeners planted fewer "soul food" crops, but they were congenial and cheerful as we all worked our allotted plots of ground. I'm convinced there's nothing better than working in the soil to relieve the mental frustrations of a pressured lifestyle such as ours.

As suggested before, one thing that made for slower church growth and new church starts in Erie was the closed minds and provincialism of the people. This is not said to discredit them. Each region of our country has its own thought and behavior patterns which determine openness to new ideas and new people.

For example, in the South, we grew up speaking to everyone we met whether we knew them or not. A friendly smile, a jaunty tipping of the hat, a wave of the hand all said, "Hi, how are you?" We had never seen them before, and may never see them again, but for that moment in time, our hearts were open to friendliness. We operated from the position that "a stranger is a friend we haven't met yet." It made for a free and easy lifestyle with a minimum of restraints on new friend-ships.

By contrast, one day I answered our door in Erie to see a well-dressed man of about forty. He was ill at ease, hesitant to respond when I spoke to him. Finally, he asked how to get to downtown Erie. I, thinking he was a newcomer to the city, started giving directions. He couldn't follow my directions because he didn't know where he was at the time. He explained he'd lived in Erie all his life, but he'd never been on our end of town. He didn't know our street, which was Sterrettania Road (Route 832). It was the main route out of Erie to pick up Interstate 90, east and west, and I 79, north and south. I couldn't believe it. I called Cornelius to come help the man. He gave him landmarks and bus routes which I didn't know. I suppose the man got home that day.

No matter where they are, Baptists need a place to baptize. If a church is growing it feels this pressure regularly. Before we built the Millcreek Church building, we sometimes baptized in Lake Erie. But in the winter we would have to *borrow* some other church's facilities. That wasn't easy because not all churches immerse their members.

Frank Borowski's baptism in Lake Erie.

One Lake Erie baptism stands out in my mind because it was different. Frank was a candidate for baptism, and he requested to be baptized out in the lake, "just like Jesus was." As a young man, Frank had lost a leg in a barroom fight, and he now wore an artificial limb. Knowing the danger of trying to walk him into the lake's soft, mushy, slimy bottom, Cornelius asked two of our deacons to wade Frank out sitting in a chair. When the time came, Cornelius baptized Frank, chair and all. He was immersed all right, and the deacons who held on felt they were, too.

I also remember Ruth's baptism because she procrastinated so long. Ruth was discovered by our summer workers doing survey. She was about fifty years old, a large woman of Polish descent. She began coming to church and soon was gloriously saved. But she put off being baptized. Cornelius didn't pressure her, just counseled her and answered her questions. Finally, about four months later, the truth came out. Ruth was afraid that Cornelius, five feet eight inches tall, weighing 160 pounds, could not baptize her, five feet eleven inches tall, weighing 220 pounds. She was terrified with the thought.

A few weeks later the problem was solved. Ruth watched Cornelius baptize a man six feet four inches tall, 260 pounds with the greatest of ease. She just couldn't believe it. She immediately asked to be baptized right away. Ruth's baptism was not only an act of obedience for her, but also a victory over her fear.

Of course every baptismal service speaks volumes to the candidate and the church. I must mention one more. The candidate was a young mother of two who had recently lost her third child to Sudden Infant Death Syndrome (SIDS). Sue genuinely accepted the Lord and wanted to turn her life around. Just the week before, she had brought me her husband's pornographic magazine collection and watched me burn them. She also threw away her cigarettes and vowed never to smoke again. Her heart was in the right place.

Imagine our surprise when Sue wore a bright red bikini for her baptism. She was completely unaware that it was not appropriate. The lady from our church, who was assisting the women candidates, rushed out into the auditorium to tell me of Sue's attire. Since our church didn't have baptismal robes, Cornelius instructed the candidates to bring complete changes of clothing and to wear something water wouldn't hurt in which to be baptized.

Sue explained, "Pastor Bright said to wear something water wouldn't hurt. What's wrong with my bathing suit?" I persuaded Sue to put her dress on for the baptismal service. Afterwards, we wrapped her warmly in towels for her trip home. (Always have plenty of huge, thirsty towels.) Sue grew to understand why her bikini was inappropriate, but at her baptism, she had been honestly confused.

Though Millcreek Church grew, it was slow. With such a weak base, reaching out to other communities was slower for us. However, we did reach out to Oil City, about thirty-five miles southeast of Erie. Oil City was about ten miles south of Titusville where the first oil well—Drake's Well—was dug in the United States. The resulting oil that flowed into and through the creek (Oil Creek) meandered through the city and gave it its name.

Ronnie Burkett, one of our 1967 summer missionaries, came back in June 1968, to lead a Bible study with the Bob Halls and the Millers. By knocking on doors and visiting prospects, Ronnie came to believe a church could be started in Oil City, if we could put a pastor on the field. He believed so strongly in the work that he transferred his college credits from Mississippi to Clarion State College, near Oil City, in order to keep working with the people. We praised God for Ronnie and thanked the Pennsylvania-South Jersey State Convention for financial support for him that year. Ronnie came to mean much to us in the Northwest Association, and even more later, in the Pittsburgh Association.

In May of 1969, Blanton and Jean Adair, and their lovely, talented daughters, came to pastor the Hasson Heights Baptist Church of Oil City. They added much to our work by way of knowledge and experience, but, most of all, they helped by their loving concern for the lost and their willingness to serve God in a difficult place. It encouraged us so much to have them in the Northwest Association.

We'd felt for a long time we needed a work in southeast Erie. We were on the west side. We made it a matter of personal prayer and concern. We did a windshield survey and felt there was, indeed, real potential for a new church start. We began mentioning the need in our monthly newsletter for our friends to pray about.

In the summer of 1970, it seemed things were coming together. Paul and Jimmie Chidester, and their five fine children, came to begin the work that became known as Southeast Erie Baptist Chapel. We were pleased that so many people and churches helped to underwrite Paul's salary. Paul had finished his work for the Doctor of Theology Degree from Southwestern Seminary, and was, without a doubt, the best educated pastor in our association. We were delighted to have the whole Chidester family working with us.

On September 6, 1970, the Southeast Baptist Chapel met for their first Sunday service. It was our joy, and our sorrow, to

The Chidester family—back row: Mark, Paul (father), and Jim; middle row: Rebecca and Lola; front row: Charis and Jimmie (mother).

have one of our best families, John and Eileen Urquhart, and son Tommy, move to the chapel. We knew we would miss them at Millcreek, but we also knew how important it is to have someone experienced in mission work to help a new church get started. I'm sure John and Eileen considered it a time of growth for them, too.

In 1971, Bolivar Drive Baptist Church in Bradford, Pennsylvania, near the New York state line in the Frontier Association, began a work in Warren, Pennsylvania. Nathan Luce led the work that became known as Pleasant Hills Baptist Chapel. They had a special ministry to the deaf in the Warren area. Sometime later, that work came under our sponsorship because they became a part of the Northwest Association. Rex and Evalyn Hatley, and son Steve, came to minister there. In time the church built a building and was renamed the Jackson Way Baptist Church.

The Polish/English Open Bible Tabernacle Baptist Church, in Erie, affiliated with the Southern Baptist Convention, and hence with us, in 1972. In May that year, they asked Cornelius to be the interim pastor. He preached there at 9:30 Sunday mornings and rushed back over the seven miles to Millcreek for the 11:00 A.M. service. Open Bible didn't have Sunday School, but Cornelius led the children and youth in Bible studies on Thursday night before their prayer service. Of course this was a demanding schedule for Cornelius, but he loved the people and was happy to serve them.

In July that year, Adam Piasechi, from Poland, came to be pastor of the Polish speaking members at Open Bible. He immediately began learning English and was progressing very well, much better than Cornelius was with Polish. They became great friends.

In the summer of 1973, Ray Franklin, son of Raymond and Irene Franklin of Newton Falls, Ohio, came to serve Open Bible as summer pastor. His coming relieved Cornelius of some of his responsibilities. That was a blessing!

Then, God truly answered our prayers and sent Tom and Alyce Adams to pastor the Open Bible Church. They led the church to reach out to Erie City—the church was close-in, nearly downtown—and to be more in line with Southern Baptist work. They also initiated a jail ministry that proved very successful. Tom spearheaded a drive to get a baptistry for the jail. It was put to use as the inmates made professions of faith. And, with the encouragement and leadership of the Open Bible Church, a new church was started in Wattsburg.

About this time, the Hasson Heights Church in Oil City began a work in the Marrianne/Clarion area. Joe and Jane McClung, with their children, came to pastor there. Slowly, but surely, progress was being made.

While we northwestern Pennsylvanians enjoyed the relationship we had with the Pittsburgh Baptist Association, we found the 150 miles too far for our people to go to associational meetings. In new work areas, the work of the association is vital to church growth. And, since we were growing, we felt we needed to become an association of churches in our area. We let our needs and desires be known. How we rejoiced when Lowell and Gladys Wright, and daughter Rebecca, came as our first Northwest Baptist Association director of missions. Now we were on our way!

One of the most exciting things that happened to us in Erie was June's wedding. She graduated from Georgetown College in Kentucky in May 1971. That summer she married James Robert Gray (Jim). He had just graduated from Hiram College in Ohio. June and Jim had been friends, then sweethearts, throughout their junior high years at Turner Junior High School and their senior high years at Warren G. Harding High School, from which they graduated in 1967. They long-distance dated the four years of college, then set the wedding date for June 19, 1971.

It was an idealistic setting—our huge manicured backyard. Cheryl Sullivan, neighbor and friend, played pre-wedding music on her flute, accompanied by her father at the piano.

June and Jim's wedding, 1971. Left to right: Art and Bonnie Gray, Jim Gray, June Bright Gray, and Edna and Cornelius Bright.

The birds were singing and the sun was shining as Cornelius walked June down the "aisle" to Jim at the decorated wedding bower. Alona, as maid of honor, and five of June's friends, as bridesmaids, dressed in vibrant lavender and purple, made a beautiful scene. The young men, groomsmen, dressed in dark pants and white coats, set off the near perfect scene.

June, in her original gown, made by a dear friend at church, let go of her father's arm and stood happily by Jim. Cornelius then performed the ceremony in a hushed atmosphere. A joyous reception followed in a special festive tent, there in the backyard. What a day!

June and Jim left for a brief honeymoon. A week later they were in Philadelphia for Peace Corps Orientation. Then they were gone for two years! They were assigned to Ghana in West Africa to teach. Jim liked it, but June decided that teaching was not her "calling." The second year they worked with the Health Ministry. They gave shots, lectured on health issues, and demonstrated basic hygiene practices. Often the work was slow, especially when vaccines were not available. However, during those slow times, June and Jim were able to see parts of the country they could not have seen otherwise.

In December 1972, Alona, Cornelius, and I paid the Grays a visit in Ghana. That adventure, and associated misadventures, would fill another book. For us, it was a dream come true. We delighted in seeing firsthand our missionaries serving on foreign soil. We will never forget the sights, sounds, and smells! Our hearts rejoiced when Dr. Jim Barron took us out to a village near Tamale and let us teach grown men to read in the Dagbani language. Women and children were not taught, but they watched in rapt attention. What a thrill that was! The men were responsive, and Dr. Barron said we did a good job. Of course we were limited, but God wasn't. He was there. We felt his presence.

When we returned home, Alona wrote a letter to her friends about the trip. Cornelius and I liked it so well we asked her to add our names as senders. Her wonderful report, expressive and colorful, follows. Enjoy Ghana!

January 10, 1973

Dear Friends,

I think it's only fair to warn you that I (Alona) wrote this letter for my friends, but when Mom read it, she said it would do for her and Dad, too, so . . . we hope you will forgive us for sending this form letter of our impressions of Ghana. We see no other way to tell you *all* about the complete trip. This may be very long, so, have a seat. Here we go!

December 14. I felt confident that things were okay at school. A good friend was taking my classes and we had pre-planned. Mom, Dad, and I were scheduled to leave Erie International Airport at 11:13 A.M. on Allegheny Airlines. Well, it was a bad week for Allegheny and they cancelled that flight. We finally got away at 3:00 P.M. THAT SHOULD HAVE BEEN TAKEN AS A BAD OMEN!!!

Arrival at LaGuardia in New York City was late because we
had to circle in a traffic pattern for thirty minutes before
landing. We missed the helicopter from LaG to Kennedy by
minutes and found ourselves panicking—with one hour to
catch our 7:00 o'clock overseas flight from Kennedy Airport.

My Medal of Honor, for the trip, goes to that New York City
cab driver who took us through NYC rush hour traffic to JFK
in 35 minutes. We made our Pan AM flight quite breathless.

The plane was a 707—biggest we'd ever flown—and nice.
The three meals served on the plane were fantastic. We flew
6 1/2 straight hours (gaining 5 clock hours in route) and
landed in Dakar, Senegal at 7 A.M. to a beautiful African
sunrise. After a short re-fueling stop, we hopped over to
Monrovia, Liberia. Layover there was long enough for us to
set foot on another country. Finally, at 12 Noon, Accra time,
we hit Ghanaian cement. As we taxied to the parking area, I
spotted June and Jim atop the observation platform, waving
madly, though they couldn't see us.

Out of the plane, we greeted the hot sun and warm smiles of
Ghana. The hassle of going through customs, and discov-
ering our luggage didn't make the trip with us, delayed our
seeing June and Jim. But, finally, bear hugs and kisses were
abundant. All five of us were ecstatic.

Our two-week Ghanain adventure was made perfect by the
wonderful planning June and Jim had done. We were in the
capital city of Accra for one day—beginning our introduction
to a fascinating country. Accra is on the coastal plains—a
beautiful setting.

My first impressions were of the vegetation. With banana and
coconut trees everywhere, and poinsettia bushes glowing, it
was really Africa and really Christmas. The heat was not
oppressive, just noticeable. The people were curious, staring
and calling "bruni" (white person) whenever we passed.

Accra is a big, bustling city. Though most cars are taxis, there are many on the roads. Most Ghanaian common folk walk, or travel by lorry (a VW van without sides) or mammy lorry (an open truck bed with 12″ wide benches about two feet apart). These are cheap transports which travel from city to city, and around town.

Ghana does have a bus system, the State Transport, which we rode from Accra to Kumasi. It is a regular bus except that, in the middle aisle, after all other seats are filled, a folddown seat is used to accommodate more people. It was a bumpy, crowded ride.

Kumasi is the capital of the Ashanti region and in the rain forest geographical area. I fell in love with the town and the people. The Ashantis have so much culture that it is unique to them. It was easy to assimilate and appreciate. This is the center of Ghana's most beautiful crafts in wood, textiles, silver, and gold. Since June and Jim lived 35 miles from Kumasi their first year, they were very familiar with the city.

We spent 3 full days in Kumasi, living in a hotel with a bathroom (tub and toilet), a toilet room (just commode), and a shower room (just a shower head in the middle of a small room), on each floor to serve 18–20 people. But it was like dormitory life and easy to adapt to. No air-conditioning in Ghana, except in exclusive places. Overhead fans are common everywhere in public places, and they *do* help.

One of the most impressive sights to Mother and me was the way thousands of Ghanaians live on the sidewalks and at the edge of the roads. They cook over open fires, sell foods they've gathered or cooked, urinate, and even sleep outside. Most do, however, have a room in which to sleep at night.

It is a peddling society. Even small children carry oranges, bananas, bread, baked plantains (large, toughish banana-like food), and fried chunks of yam (like white potatoes) to sell for a few pesewas (equiv. of pennies). Most carrying is done in large baskets or in trays balanced on the head. (Hope you're still with me. Rest a minute.)

Small children are carried on their mother's back, being tied there by a large piece of cloth tucked tightly in front. Most women I noticed were pregnant, or had a small child in tow. Life span is about fifty.

In large cities, men, women, and children are fully clothed—some in western dress and others in Ghanaian. The cities are crowded, but the colors in the crowds seem so much richer than in the United States. I think the rich, brown body color of the Ghanaian makes the reds, greens, blues, and yellows much more vivid than on white "washed out" skin. Most Ghanaians are dark. There wasn't the high percentage of light-skinned people as in American Blacks.

We attended church at Grace Baptist Church in Kumasi on Dec. 17. It was an English speaking church and was very much like any large church in the United States. We sang the same songs, and prayed to the same Lord. The building just had screens over the windows and the breeze across the congregation was very helpful in worship. Daddy spoke that morning and did a good job.

Before leaving Kumasi, June and Daddy went down to pick up our luggage in Accra. They flew Ghana Airways. Everything was there and in good shape. It was good to see some clothes. Mom and I each bought a Ghanaian dress on Saturday to have for church on Sunday. They are beautiful, typically Ghanaian with intricate needlework at the neck and cuffs. Our luggage came Monday, three days after we did.

On Tuesday, December 19, we took a lorry (a real experience in itself) 35 miles out to Dompoase, a little village where J. and J. lived before, when they taught at Dompoase Training

College. The people were very friendly, and we could tell they thought a lot of J. and J. We saw the compound where they lived.

We also saw the outside toilet in the middle of the compound which usually had feces flung on the wall. (Note: Ghanaians, in the bush, clean themselves with their left hands . . . no toilet paper . . . or corncobs . . . or Sears catalogues! This is why they *never* give you anything with the left hand. Even when clean, it is considered unclean because of the purpose for which it is used.) June had real problems relaxing in such a situation and developed a spastic colon. Since moving to Tamale, and having their own inside flush toilet, this problem has cleared up.

On Wednesday, we rode the State Transport to Tamale, 238 miles north, which took eight hours. We stopped along the road several times, at the discretion of the driver. We arrived at the Volta River Lake just as the ferry was loading, so there was no wait there. It took one hour to cross the river/lake, then we continued by bus.

Tamale is a very different area. It also is a large city, but the geographical region is the northern plain, covered with inhospitable scrub. This time of the year the plains were dry and dusty—a wilderness.

The small villages in the Northern Region are round mud huts—unlike the rain forest homes of adobe brick with tin roofs. These villages really looked like the Africa I'd pictured since I was a child.

The Northerners are mainly Moslem. This accounts for the differences in dress, culture, and, of course, religious practices. Evangelical mission groups are growing in the North. Presbyterians and Catholics are making great inroads. Baptists are new in the North but are growing slowly. Baptist mission work in other parts of Ghana is strong.

It was good to get home to Tamale and June and Jim's house, to be able to relax and visit more. Their houseboy, Atia, was shy but friendly. He had kept the house safe from "teeves" while they were away. (They'd been robbed twice before getting Atia.)

June and Jim's house was built by Russians about ten years before, as a home for Russian Advisors in Ghana. All the houses in their section of the city are now used by high government officials and Peace Corps personnel. It's a good house like many upperclass Ghanaians have. It had two bedrooms, a large living-dining area, a bathroom with tub and shower, and a kitchen.

In Tamale, we were amazed by the market . . . several blocks of peddlers selling all kinds of food, housewares, clothing, and other goods. The sights and smells of the market were indescribable to say the least.

The foods in Ghana were easy to eat. The staples were rice, yams, plantains, and groundnuts (peanuts). Fish also made up a large part of the diet. We had no trouble adapting, except for the highly seasoned (peppered) sauces and soups. The main drink of the country is beer—much more potent than American brands. Cokes are available and are called minerals. Water in the cities is good, but we didn't trust it out in the country. June is a good cook, so we were kept happy in that respect.

Jim went out in the yard and cut a palm tree branch which served as a tropical Christmas tree. It was decorated with homemade ornaments. The effect wasn't exactly a Pennsylvania style Christmas tree, but it was wonderful. We'd taken wrapping paper in our luggage, so the gifts looked Christmas—y, too.

While up north, we went a little further, to Nalerigu, where we have a Baptist hospital. It is known as the best hospital in Ghana, and as good as any other in West Africa. We were impressed by the missionaries we met there. Fantastic people!

Willie Mae Berry, from Georgia, a nurse at the hospital, gave us a huge white rooster for Christmas dinner. That was a wonderful gift because a good-sized fowl is hard to come by in Ghana. And he sure did taste good stuffed with cornbread dressing.

Christmas Eve we attended a combined carol sing and Scripture reading with the Jim Barrons, one of our missionary families. It was held at a large Presbyterian church in Tamale. The service was truly inspiring as nine church choirs sang beautiful anthems. The Lord lives in Ghana, too!!!

I guess the most exciting and memorable portion of our trip, for me, was when we went with Jim Barron to a small mud hut village and helped some men learn to read in the Dagbani language. Dr. Barron goes twice weekly to hold reading classes and Bible Study there. Two young men, who are Baptist Pastor's School students, help him.

It was a thrill, and I guess the teacher in me could relate to that kind of missionary work. The Wycliffe Bible Translators have people in the Northern Region translating the whole Bible into the Dagbani language. It is a *newly written* language but the sounds are like English which is Ghana's official language. Except for three or four peculiar sounds of special symbols, it was easy to listen to these men, young and old, read. I re-live that afternoon often.

Other general impressions? I felt very safe on any street we traveled in Ghana. We walked quite a bit and I wasn't afraid. Every person we met was friendly and helpful.

Except for in the Kumasi Zoo, we didn't see any wild animals. We only saw cows, goats (status symbols for villages, not eaten in great numbers), and chickens. We were not in the animal rich East African countries, but Ghana has her riches, too.

Besides having June and Jim for two years, Ghana owns gold, silver, diamonds, and cocoa. These are major exports. They are the world's third largest producer of cocoa, and have one of the largest diamond mines in the world. The textile industry is big, too. Cloth (100% cotton) is bright and beautiful. It is made in Ghana, woven and dyed there, from imported cotton. I loved the African colors.

Sadly, but of necessity, we left Ghana on Dec. 28th, for Paris. We spent a fantastic day and night there. We ate a sunnyside-up breakfast at 10 A.M. (That *becomes* important.) We toured the city and loved it!

Flying from Paris to London on the 29th, we began the most harrowing part of our journey. After the plane began a landing pattern in London, we had to pull up and return to Paris because of the LONDON FOG! That was a prediction of things to come.

After a mad rush from the airport to the train depot, barely making it, we got the 10 P.M. train to London. It went across the French countryside to Dunkurque. There was no food or water on the train, and we had last eaten at 10 A.M.

Surprisingly, at one of those little podunk stations in the middle of nowhere, we heard familiar-sounding voices. When several people got on the train there, I invited a girl to sit by us because she sounded like a hometown Alabamian. Yes, she and her husband were from Birmingham, Alabama; East Lake, in fact. His parents live only two blocks from where we lived in Birmingham. He and Daddy had attended the same college, were even there one year together. Amazing! The world *is* tiny. We had a nice visit as the wheels clattered. I guess we have friends all over the world, some of whom we haven't met yet.

At Dunkurque, we detrained, got on a ferry for a five hour ride, at 7 A.M. de-ferried, and finally got to London at 9:30. It had been a twelve hour ordeal. That Parisian breakfast had long since run out, but after finding a good hotel and getting food, we began to recover from our period of weakness.

The fog didn't lift the days we were in London. On our tour out in the country to Windsor Castle, our guide *told* us we were looking at a formidable building, but the fog was so thick we couldn't see so much as an outline. We bought some ready-made slides so we could show others, as well as ourselves, where we were, and what we were supposed to have seen.

As a consequence of the ghastly fog, our scheduled flight out of London on January 1, was cancelled. All 300 of us passengers were put up in a luxury hotel for the night. Mom and I called our principals to let them know we would not be in school on the 2nd.

As our big 747 (what a plane!) lifted off at 4 P.M. the next afternoon, the whole planeload of happy folk clapped and cheered. It was a wonderful flight to New York's JFK.

We got the helicopter ride from Kennedy to LaGuardia this time. That was a thrill, too, but when we got to New York, there were no more planes to Erie. We ran to catch a flight to Cleveland, rented a car, and drove home to Erie, arriving at 1 A.M. January 3rd. It had been a long adventure, and the last leg had taken its toll on us physically. But we would not trade the trip for anything.

I know you're tired of reading, and even with this volume, I feel I haven't adequately described the world on the other side. The miracles and beauties of this world, and the people of this world, never cease to amaze me. The impression left on my heart is that people are people, and God is God, wherever

you are. And God and man living in harmony is a beautiful
sight anywhere!

When we see you folks, we have about 650 slides to show, so
be prepared!!!

Thanks for the time.

Love,
Alona, Edna, and Cornelius

Now back to the real world—*Erie* and the work God called
us to do.

Not every church start continues and matures into a strong,
viable ministry station. We believe all are begun in prayer and
with a deep desire to meet spiritual needs. We know the hearts
of those who set out to lead a new work are dedicated to
making the work succeed, but sometimes it doesn't. We don't
know why this is true, only that it is heartbreaking when it
happens. Deep heartsearching follows each church *stop.*

Possible reasons for a new church faltering and eventually
closing its doors include: 1) poor timing of the start; 2) poor
location for meeting place; 3) wrong choice of leader/pastor;
4) lack of concern and commitment of sponsoring church;
5) shifts in the economy; 6) lack of financial support for the
pastor; and 7) lack of prayer support from God's people.

We encouraged our friends to pray for the churches we
helped to start. We trust they did. Month after month we sent a
newsletter to over two hundred friends who had asked to be put
on our mailing list. We seldom had time for personal letters, but
we always tried to get our newsletter out every month.

The following is an example, verbatim, of one of our
newsletters. This one was mailed on May 8, 1973. It was saved
and offered to me by Paul and Jimmie Chidester. I am so
thankful they gave me this particular letter. It helps us to
understand their struggle in giving up the Southeast Chapel.
They returned to Georgia sometime after this letter was

written. (They are now working for the Lord in their church in Macon, Georgia.) The Newsletter:

4641 Sterrettania Road
Erie, Pennsylvania
May 8, 1973

Greetings:

We love you. We wish we could write each of you a special note telling you how very deeply we appreciate your prayers and your material support. Since that is impossible, please think of this newsletter as personally to you, from us, with warmest regards.

June and Jim have about seven weeks to go in Ghana. They are excited and so are we. We are hoping to have a reception for them when they get home. It'll be almost like a reception for newlyweds, returning from their honeymoon, since they left for Ghana about 2 1/2 weeks after they were married. How we wish all of you could be here to share in our joy at their return.

Let's see now if I can catch you up on us. Cornelius sure had a busy March and April. In addition to his regular work as pastor of Millcreek and Open Bible Churches, he had a one night speaking engagement in the First Baptist Church of Jeffersontown, Kentucky, on March 7th. He was in a World Missions Conference in Marshall County, Alabama, March 18–25. He was in a revival with Laurel Baptist Church in Uniontown, PA April 9–15. During all of this he was trying to get our church construction loan—being refused by one bank—but approved by another. He has really been putting in the hours, 12–16 a day for weeks on end.

Alona is another Bright who has been very busy. Besides teaching eighth graders, she works with our Zone III Youth Choir, "The Fellowmen." They had a performance in March at the Hasson Heights Church in Oil City. Their musical, "It's All About Love" is done very well, indeed. They had a performance at Marrianne last Saturday night, and will have one next Sunday night at the Austin Village Baptist Church in Warren, Ohio.

Most of you know how much time and effort it takes for the leader to accomplish something like this and make it worthwhile. They meet monthly for fun, fellowship, inspiration, and practice. How pleased we are with this fine group of young people from our Zone III churches, and with Alona for her good spirit and hard work.

March and April found Edna teaching third graders, serving as PTA Spiritual Life Chairman, meeting with the GAs, and accompanying them on their mission action project, planning and hosting the children and preschool Easter parties, visiting elderly, homebound folks, recuperating from a fall she had on a downtown street, recovering from a week long bout with laryngitis, *and* entertaining guests.

We had company over Easter weekend from LaPorte, Indiana. The T. Bentley Warringtons, seminary friends of ours, came on Friday and stayed until Monday. They helped us have a record attendance on *Easter Sunday—62.*

We regret the sad news we have concerning the work on the Southeast side of Erie. In the last news letter, we mentioned the chapel had given up their renting of the $200.00 a month store building, and had begun a home fellowship type ministry. They had three such Bible Study groups but Brother Chidester didn't feel they were reaching new people. He turned in his resignation, as mission pastor, to our missions committee, effective June first.

They, the Chidesters, have had added complications due to a broken ankle Mrs. Chidester sustained in a fall on the ice as she was going to work one night. (She is a nurse.) She has not been able to return to work, but does seem to be recovering nicely now. We ask your continued prayers for the Chidesters as they seek God's will for their lives at this time.

Now, to switch to a cheerier note. We, Millcreek Baptist Church, did reach our Annie Armstrong Easter Offering Goal of $231.44. We thank God for that. The need is so great, and some of our people realize it. Hence, they gave generously.

AND, the Builders for Christ will be here to help us the week of July 1–7. Our men are working hard—trying to get all done, that needs to be done, before George Carkeet and the Builders get here. In one week's time, they will put our building up. DO YOU WANT TO HELP? If so, let us, or Bro. Carkeet know. Address him at P.O. Box 38, Greenwood, Louisiana, 71033. His phone number is (318) 936-5358. We will be glad to provide food and shelter while you are here. Let us know as early as possible.

Isn't it exciting to think that the men and their families will give one week of their vacation to help us build our church building? We will provide the materials for the work, food, and shelter for the men and their families, and they will provide the labor and *know how*. Pray for them as they make this journey to us, for the work they will be doing, and for all of us as we give God the glory for everything that is accomplished.

We received two members in April, one by letter and the other on profession of faith. And, last Sunday, (first Sunday in May) we had a fine young family join—Mac and Ann Davis and their daughter Beth. They also have two younger daughters who joined our Sunday School. God continues to work. He always will, if we'll just let him.

STATISTICALLY this is us for March and April—averaged together, SS—36, MW—42, CT—21—, EW—23—PM—16.

The average weekly offering was $192.00.

OUTSIDE GIFTS:

For Southeast Chapel

1st Baptist Miamisburg $75.00

San Lando Springs Bapt. 100.00
  (for 2 mo.)
  Bill Hyde 20.00
  Bill & Shirley Crews 36.00

For Millcreek

H. L. Cockrell $25.00

4th Avenue, B'ham 200.00
S. A. Beall 5.00
Gloria Wooten 5.00
W. A. Brown 5.00

DEAR FRIENDS: Please consider our invitation to come and help us while the Builders for Christ are here, July 1–7. You will never be the same, we promise. Nor will we. We'll all be better for the experience of working together.

LOVE,
Edna, Cornelius, and Alona

It would be good if every pastor in the deep South could serve in a new church in a pioneer area for a short time. They'd soon see that the sacrifices the men and their families make to start and ground a new church are significant and very real. The normal challenges of educating children, paying for health care, and building buildings seem to double when you don't have the cushion of family, friends, and fellow Christians around you. It takes a special kind of family to go to those less evangelized, less churched, and less interested people, and carry out the Great Commission.

It's relatively easy to grow a church in the South where everybody knows what it means to be "born again," where even the Methodists know Baptist doctrine, where most people believe only Christ can save souls, and where it's easy to lead programs when you have dozens of pastor friends promoting the same things. It's like having a *big* family with everyone willing to help.

But, for the lone pastor and his family, a new work in an unevangelized area can be very lonely. However, you can believe me when I say the men and women (and children) we knew never considered it a sacrifice. They rejoiced in serving the Lord, even in difficult times and in rough places. No, they were not super Christians. They were just ordinary people whose vision of serving an extraordinary God captured them. Their willingness to have less, materially, gained for them great spiritual rewards.

The Millcreek Church in Erie helped start, or stabilize, nine churches the ten and a half years we were there. God did mighty works to get the churches going. Sometimes, some of the first members (thank God not all) abandoned ship when new people came in and started working in the churches. This phenomenon is not unusual, just strange. It could be caused by jealousy or envy. We always felt it was due to immaturity.

When the first members feel they own (possess) the church, newcomers are a threat to them. In their frustration of losing control, or status, they sometimes bail out and move on. It's always a loss to the church when they go, but it's a greater loss to them. They tend to become "church hoppers"—not a good thing, and certainly not a positive Christian witness.

When leaders in young churches move to follow their jobs, or to retire back home, the congregations can be overwhelmed with the losses, both of leadership and finances. It takes time and wise, committed pastoral leadership to restore confidence, regain losses, and "regroup the troops." But, it can be done. When it does happen, the struggles make believers stronger because they remember who they are and whom they serve.

June and Jim came home from Ghana, visited us a while, then took off for Grand Island, Nebraska, where they were assigned in the Vista Program. They, along with eight to ten other Vista people, renovated an old church building, making it a community center. Later, out of the Vista Program, Jim studied for his Master's Degree in Education at the University of Nebraska at Kearney. June was busy working in a hospital and a nursing home. She enjoyed both. That may have been instrumental in her later specializing in mental health in Pittsburgh, where they moved from Grand Island.

CHAPTER 5

Look Around — Miracles Abound

IT WAS IN 1977, AT THE PENNSYLVANIA-SOUTH JERSEY State Convention, that Dr. G. W. Bullard, executive secretary, and Jack Smith, director of missions for the Northeast Association, asked Cornelius if he'd be interested in going to eastern Pennsylvania to be the pastor of Conyngham Valley Baptist Church. He would be the pastor and would start churches "on the side." Cornelius told me of that conversation. He gave them no answer.

The work at Millcreek had stabilized. I had quit teaching to be more available for the church work. Alona was teaching at Waterford and had moved into her own apartment. June and Jim had settled in Pittsburgh and become parents. It might be a good time to consider a move.

We prayed, as usual, but this time even harder. The Millcreek Church was growing, and we felt it was on solid ground. But, we had several new Christians who needed extra time, care, and attention. This was the first time we'd had positive responses from some young people, in the drug culture, to whom we had witnessed. We feared they would feel abandoned if we left. We dreaded leaving them. It was sort of like moving off and leaving your children.

But, here again, we knew God would provide for them. It was his work, not ours. The new converts were his children, and he would meet their needs. The Lord gave us peace that we should go.

Cornelius told Jack Smith that we would move to northeastern Pennsylvania. Truthfully, I was looking forward to a situation where we'd already have a church building. We wouldn't have to start from scratch, as we'd always done before. What would it be like? What parameters had already been set—that I would have to fit into? What would be expected of, and from, me? I was eager to find out.

Conyngham Valley Baptist Church welcomed us with open arms. Our first Sunday, they had a "calling of the roll." Each family stood as they were introduced to us, and, if they wanted to, gave us a personal welcome. We liked that. They made us feel wanted and needed. At first, I didn't realize how much. There had been "trouble" in the church, and feelings had been hurt. The differing factions openly, verbally attacked each other in business meetings. The young pastor had resigned because the deacons couldn't/wouldn't work together. It was a sad state of affairs.

One of Cornelius's spiritual gifts was the ability to help people resolve their differences. I later teased Dr. Bullard about that being the reason he and Jack Smith approached Cornelius about going to Conyngham. He laughed and said that was just one of the reasons.

Perhaps another reason Dr. Bullard wanted us in Conyngham was to host the Pennsylvania-South Jersey State Convention in November that year—1977. That we did, just two months after we arrived in Conyngham. Looking back, I know that was a *big* undertaking, but then, it was just something that needed to be done. We, in northeastern Pennsylvania, needed the attention and recognition the Convention brought to our association, the newest in the state.

The Sunday before we arrived in Conyngham, one of the disgruntled deacons left the church. We never knew him. Before long, the others settled down, and the healing process began.

The church, which was small, about fifty-five members, had bought a beautiful, old Lutheran church building. It was much larger than needed but proved a great blessing when we hosted the Convention.

Because we started growing, and because of our past trials and tribulations in finding places to baptize, the first thing Cornelius wanted to do was put in a baptistry. Several of the older members didn't approve taking out the life-sized pictures of two of the apostles behind the pulpit. (Remember the church was built for Lutherans.)

Cornelius explained how and where the baptistry would be placed. The pictures would have to go. Since we were Baptists, it seemed the pictures should not prevent our having a place to baptize. Agreement was reached, and soon we were in the baptizing business.

The auditorium was quite large with a huge "empty" space in the back. The building committee drew up plans to make church offices there. The existing office was a tiny room in the basement, hardly accessible, and not good for books and equipment. The new offices were truly a blessing. We were all proud of them.

One area in this church, about which we couldn't complain, was the kitchen. The equipment was old but in excellent condition. The kitchen was just off the large dining/social hall area. We used that space frequently, not just with our own congregation, but for the many large groups that came to help us. The miracles of coordination and cooperation among the church groups who came were amazing. But then, God's people are supposed to be able to work together. It is always a thrill to see God work, out in the field where the harvest is plentiful, *or* in the kitchen, where the work sometimes goes unnoticed. Cornelius and I often thanked God for the churches who sent us their best people. What joy they brought to our busy lives.

The Valley Baptist Church was growing, and we were kept busy with the works already begun. The Hometown Church was relocated to Tamaqua and became known as the Tamaqua

Baptist Church. Dudley and Dottie Penton came to pastor there. They also worked with the Park Place Church and helped us start in Pottsville, southeast of Tamaqua.

The church in Berwick, where Ron and Pam Windle pastored, helped start the Bloomsburg Church. Oh, the beauty of working with dedicated men and women. There was always a willingness to pitch in and help. Jack Smith, our director of missions, felt every church should have a mission. That was our goal. The Wilks Barre Church was started by Jack Smith, himself, leading it. How strong and sweet the fellowship was in the Northeast Baptist Association.

One of the special joys Cornelius and I had at Conyngham was participating in the two nursing home ministries the Valley Church had going. Juanita Pollard, our church pianist, went faithfully to the Butler Valley Nursing Home and played the piano for hymn singing. Afterwards, Cornelius spoke, and then we'd visit with the residents. We always tried to visit the ones in their rooms, too.

The other home was the Sparr Nursing Home, down in the valley. Cornelius and I went every Wednesday for Bible study. What a pleasure it was to minister to these aging saints, and how appreciative they, and the staff, were.

Another ongoing work was the Scranton Polish/English afternoon service once a month, usually the fourth Sunday. Most of the people spoke English, so Cornelius didn't try to use the limited Polish he'd learned in Erie. The Scranton folks insisted on serving us a light supper before we headed back to Conyngham—about sixty miles—for the evening service. We didn't have to do that too long before Jack Smith got another work going in Scranton. The leaders were able to take over the Polish service. We loved those dear folks very much.

After we'd been in Conyngham about six months, I learned the *real reason* for our being there. It was God's reason, as well as Dr. Bullard's and Jack Smith's. The cities of Hazleton and West Hazleton, on top of the mountain, just off Interstate 81, had no Southern Baptist witness. That fact didn't sit well with church planters Jack Smith and Cornelius Bright.

I was aware that Cornelius was visiting and making contacts in both cities, but I didn't know he and Jack Smith had a daring vision of doing what hadn't been done before. Time and again, I learned later, different church groups had tried to break into the closed ranks of Hazleton and West Hazleton and start a church. They had always failed. We just couldn't believe that many people didn't need a witness.

The title, and I hope the essence of this book, is GOD USES ORDINARY PEOPLE. I wrote a true, step-by-step account of the planting of the Crusade Baptist Church in Hazleton, Pennsylvania. Some names have been changed, but the people were real, and the events are documented, just as I wrote the story. God used hundreds of people, ordinary, run-of-the-mill people, to bring this church into being. I can't tell you about everybody, but I must tell you about Arnice Sims of Albertville, Alabama. At seventy plus years, Arnice came to help us in Backyard Bible Clubs (BBC) in Hazleton. Her generous support helped the church buy its first property. I thank God for dear Christian friends like Arnice Sims.

And there were Joe and Margaret Coon, friends from Birmingham days who now lived in Stone Mountain, Georgia. They were members of Indian Creek Baptist Church. They led hundreds in their church to be prayer partners with us for the Hazleton work. They prayed before, during, and after the crusade. And Joe and Margaret came to help us with surveys and soul-winning visitation. We thanked God for them and their church.

My story of the birth of Crusade Baptist follows. As you read, I hope you enjoy it and think how you can be available to go and do likewise.

PLANT A CHURCH—EXTEND THE KINGDOM

My eyes darted from Majestic Sugarloaf Mountain, rising out of the valley floor, to the autumnal blaze of Butler Mountain at the "Top of the Eighties," where Interstates 80 and 81 intersect. I sighed with contentment as Cornelius declared, "Six months ago this place was just a spot on the map, nestled in the foothills of the Pocono Mountains. Now, beautiful Conyngham Valley is our home."

Our neighbors, Sam and Jan Jarusek, invited us over for coffee. "What on earth is a church planter?" Jan began. "We've heard you and Edna are involved. How does one go about planting a church anyway?"

Cornelius smiled, happy to respond. "It depends on the denomination, Jan. For Baptists, the starting place is to find an underchurched area and begin there."

Sam broke in, "What does *underchurched* mean?"

"Just suppose, Sam," Cornelius explained, "that all the people who belong to all the churches in this area were present, in church, on any given Sunday. Yet, on that same Sunday, hundreds of people in this area were not in any church. We'd feel this is an underchurched area. We'd zero in on pockets of unchurched people, take a survey to determine interest level, and go from there. Summer students and mission teams help us make the survey."

"After the survey, you just set up a church and expect people to come?" Sam asked.

"Of course not," Cornelius replied. "When we find an unchurched, or underchurched, area, we pray about it. We ask our friends to join us in prayer for that specific community. We believe God answers such intercessory prayers."

"But Reverend Bright," Jan chimed in, "how do you know the unchurched people want to be Baptists?"

"We don't push being Baptists," he explained. "We base our teachings and our programs on the Bible."

Jan pushed harder. "But you do want to plant a *Baptist* church, right?"

"Yes, we do," Cornelius admitted, "but our main concern is to present the gospel so that people can make the decision to become Christians. Once that happens, they make their own choice of denomination."

"It all sounds very nice, Reverend Bright," Sam said. "But I'm sure we don't need any more churches. Look at all the churches here in the valley, and those big ones up in the city."

"Sam's right, Reverend Bright," Jan agreed. "I don't believe you can start a church here. Several times other groups have tried, only to fail. We're an older, established, predominately Catholic population. We've always been closed to new groups coming in. I'd say the chance of planting a church in Hazleton is next to nil. And, besides, what can just two people do, you and Edna?"

Cornelius smiled. "We'll leave that up to God."

I leaned forward and said, "Jan, if the Lord wants a church in the city of Hazleton, and he chooses to use us to start it, it will happen. People from churches in the South will come to help and will multiply our efforts many times over."

We stood to leave. Jan took our hands and smiled half-heartedly. She said with resignation, "Well, I guess the Lord does work in mysterious ways. God bless you."

We moved to the door where Sam patted Cornelius on the shoulder and smiled at me, then bade us good-bye. We knew our neighbors had their doubts. But we also knew God, and with him all things are possible.

Soon afterwards, Cornelius approached Hazleton's mayor about our mission teams doing door-to-door surveying. "These are the questions we will ask," Cornelius said, handing the list to the mayor.

He read the list aloud. "Do you attend a local church? If so, its name? If not, what is your denominational preference? Would you be interested in a new church in Hazleton?"

The mayor said, "I have no problem with those questions, Reverend Bright. Go ahead with your survey."

That same week, Jack Smith came for a visit. Pleased with the survey, Jack said, "We must get the city's attention. Hazleton needs to know what we are up to."

We decided to start with a tent crusade in August. We immediately began calling key people to enlist their participation. We asked Dr. James Smith, then Director of SBC Brotherhood Commission, to be our preacher. Dudley Penton, pastor of the Tamaqua Baptist Church, would coordinate the music. We notified the mission teams to come on a staggered

At Conyngham Valley Baptist Church—Left to right: Caroline Fields, a member; Jack Smith, director of missions for Northeast Association; and Connie, a friend.

schedule to help us before, during, and after the crusade.

A week later, Cornelius proudly announced, "The tent is ordered, the preacher is committed, and the mission teams are scheduled. And, much of the music is planned. Now it's time to go to work on the local level where it counts most."

The next morning, we sat in a booth at the Blue Comet Diner, waiting for its owner, Nick Ricco. Nick had a lease on the property we wanted for the crusade. City officials discouraged our asking Nick for use of the property. "He's an ex-mafia member," one whispered. "His bitter memories make him hard to deal with."

We weren't afraid. We waited for Nick.

Nick rushed in ten minutes late, hurried over to apologize, and introduced himself. While Nick caught his breath, Cornelius began. "Mr. Ricco, we want to have a tent crusade on your property across the street, the first week of August."

"A what?" Nick sputtered.

"A crusade," Cornelius explained. "It's a series of meetings to preach the gospel under a large tent. We want to put the tent on your lot. We need your permission. There will be a lot of coming and going, but no damage to the property."

"Mr. Ricco," I said, "we'll pay whatever you consider fair."

Rubbing his chin and squirming Nick said, "No, it's not that. I just don't want to be liable for injuries, accidents, losses, and stuff like that."

"You won't be," Cornelius assured Nick.

"And you'll clean up the place after the crusade?"

"Yes, of course."

Nick left the booth and made a phone call. Moments later he returned, propped his foot on the booth seat, and said, "You can use my property, the first week of August, for the sum of one dollar."

Cornelius jumped to his feet, grabbed Nick's hand, and shook it vigorously. "You won't regret it, I promise," he said.

That was the first of many miracles relating to the Hazleton crusade. In the next week, Cornelius stopped by to see the Chief of Police. "Mr. Ricco gave us permission to use his lot for our crusade," he began. "We'll need traffic control for the week. Of course we'll pay the men for overtime."

"No need of that," the chief said. "We'll provide ample protection. Good luck with your crusade."

When the mission teams confirmed their arrival times, we made reservations for them at the dorms of the Penn State Hazleton Campus. The charges were minimal, just enough to cover maintenance, housekeeping, and utilities. It certainly wasn't a money-making venture for Penn State, but it was a definite blessing to our mission teams.

When Cornelius asked the mayor if we could do a saturation witness blitz of the city, one week prior to the crusade, he explained, "This is different from the survey we did earlier. In this effort, our mission team members will give their personal testimony to the people who are interested."

The mayor agreed to the blitz and then said, "Reverend Bright, I'm for you and your people in this crusade. In fact, I'm going to proclaim Saturday Greater Hazleton *Jesus Now* Crusade Day. We'll block off Main Street, let our merchants have sidewalk sales, and let your people visit our people unobstructed by traffic. What do you think of that?"

"I'm overwhelmed, but very grateful," Cornelius answered. "Thank you, Mayor!" As he left the mayor's office, Cornelius wondered how many more miracles God would do to prepare Hazleton for the crusade.

The mission teams began arriving two weeks before the crusade started. "We do this every year," one man said. "I spend my vacation helping start churches. It's great for my whole family."

The man's wife added, "Some years our children are in Vacation Bible School and Backyard Bible Clubs four or five times. It's fun for them because they make new friends and get to see different parts of the country. Of course, it's work for me, but I love having my family together, doing mission work."

When the tent arrived, excitement filled the city. Strangers rushed over to help raise it, while shoppers stopped to watch it take shape. They marvelled as the lights were strung and the platform, chairs, piano, and sound system were all set up.

The crowds not only watched, they questioned. Who are these Southern Baptists? What are they going to do in that tent? Why are all of these out-of-state cars in town? What's going on?

Early Sunday evening, people began to gather for the first service of the crusade. The familiar hymns seemed to please the crowd and put them in a receptive mood. That night, Dr. Smith preached a stirring, but simple, message on the nature of God. Attention was focused on the speaker, and the Spirit seemed to pervade the audience. But, when the invitation was given at the conclusion, no decisions were made.

On the next night, Monday, the enthusiastic choir music welcomed the growing numbers to the service. Excitement grew as the people joined in the joyful singing of the congregational hymns. When Dr. Smith stood to speak, the crowd gave rapt attention. His message explored the depths of God's love. But, again, the invitation brought no response.

On Tuesday night, Cornelius spoke before the worship service began. "This is a new experience for many of you," he explained. "You may not know what you need to do at the conclusion when Dr. Smith extends the invitation. That is the time when, if the Holy Spirit leads you, you may choose to accept Christ as your Savior and confess him before people. We are not here to make Baptists of you, but we are here to present the gospel, to help you come to know Christ."

Seven people made professions that night. In each succeeding service, commitments were made to Christ. Attendance remained high, and on Saturday night Dr. Smith said, "We will have a worship service tomorrow morning in the lecture hall of the college across the street. If you already have a church, please go to it. The rest of you feel free to come to the lecture hall at 11:00 A.M. for our service."

The next morning, when he had concluded his sermon, Dr. Smith spoke to the congregation. "Many of you made decisions to accept Christ as your Savior this week. We thank God for your decisions. We want to encourage you to grow in your new-found faith through Bible study and prayer. The best way for you to do that is to become a member of a local church and attend it faithfully. You may want to become a charter member of the church being born here today."

Dr. Smith paused, then said, "If you are a Christian, and if you want to become a member of the Crusade Baptist Church, please come forward as we sing the invitation hymn."

Without hesitation, nine people stepped forward and were accepted as candidates for baptism. Another hymn was sung and Steve Nerger, a young ministerial student, wept, saying aloud, "God promised me there would be ten."

Dr. Smith said, "Don't you think the pastor should join, also?"

"So few," one observer remarked, "after all the work you people did. How can ten people be a church?"

"Oh, but you don't understand," Cornelius said. "All over this city more than 250 people made decisions this week, either to accept Christ as Savior or to rededicate their lives to him. Hazleton will never be the same. This is only the beginning."

Jack Smith joined in. "Rejoice! A great victory has been won. The gospel was preached, and some believed. In time, a great church will rise from all these efforts."

"And that's not all," Dr. Smith declared. "Every person who helped in this crusade is a better person for doing so. I know I am. It's been a special blessing to Nona and me."

Long ago, Steve Nerger, the young ministerial student from Southeastern Seminary in Wake Forest, North Carolina, felt God's call to missions. Now he knew Hazleton would be his field. He offered himself as pastor for the newborn church. He moved his family to Hazleton and commuted to the seminary to finish his last year.

Almost immediately, Cornelius found a church building for sale for $58,000 dollars. He and Steve, working with the pastor of that church, offered to buy it for $25,000. The pastor laughed and said, "No way! We have to get enough out of this one to help pay for our new building."

Later that same week, the pastor called Cornelius. "We'll sell our building for $25,000 if the Crusade Church will pay cash by October 15," he said.

"How on earth can we accept such a challenge?" Steve muttered when Cornelius told him. "I didn't dream he'd take us up on our offer."

"Steve," Cornelius said, "didn't we make that offer in good faith?"

"Yes," Steve groaned, "but where will we get the money?"

"The cattle on a thousand hills are his, Steve. Everything belongs to God."

"I know, I believe *that*," Steve replied, "but where can we get $25,000 by October 15?"

"First, we'll pray," Cornelius said, "and if God so leads, we'll let our friends know we need the money."

Amazed at Cornelius's faith, Steve knelt with him to pray. He ended his prayer with, "I thank you, God, for this man of faith, who takes you at your word. Help me to have faith like that."

The response to the letter we sent to our friends was incredible. October 15 came, and Steve declared to the surprised pastor, "It is with great joy that I present this check for $25,000 to you."

Cornelius watched as the elated pastor clapped his hands and near-shouted, "Praise the Lord! Now we can pay for our carpet."

Soon afterwards, the building was dedicated, as we like to say "to the glory of God and the salvation of man." At that dedicatory service, Steve stood, tears streaming down his face, and said, "We must never doubt God. He prompted Christians far removed from us, physically, to give money so we can have this building. He caused many to come to Hazleton to help us, to bring us to this high and holy hour. What a great God we serve!"

Sam and Jan Jarusek had watched every move we'd made that summer. Soon after the new church was dedicated, they wanted to give us all the credit. Sam insisted, "Nobody else could have done what you two did. The past six months have been amazing."

"No one else needed to do it, Sam," Cornelius said. "God called Edna and me to plant churches. Crusade is just one of many we have helped start. But you are right, Sam. The last six months have been amazing. We serve an amazing God. He gets things done. We're delighted he sometimes uses us in his plans. We are happy and thankful we serve a God who uses all his children to extend his Kingdom. Nothing is impossible for him. We need only to be available and respond when he calls."

Our ministry in church planting was always prefaced by much prayer and seeking God's will. The multitudes who came to help us—choir and mission groups, summer missionaries, individuals, work teams—often made the difference in the success of new church starts. So many came to help us over the years that I can't possibly name them all, but when I pray, their names and faces still come before me, and I thank God all over again. I am eternally grateful that God let us work with so many of his finest people. He knows their every sacrifice, and he rewards them!

While a different set of dynamics emerge with every new church start, there is always the same sense of drama, the same acceptance and understanding of its being of God—a miracle. God once more invades human lives and brings salvation to those who believe. Where there was no local "Body of Christ," now there is one. All of it happens because God's people believe his Word and pray, go, give, and serve. That's what keeps church planters enthusiastic.

We were happy in Conyngham. We made lifetime friends while there. Among these were Gerald and Millie Adams, our next door neighbors in Valley View Manor. When we first visited them, we learned they were Quakers. In fact, Millie's dad was a Quaker pastor. We invited them to Valley Baptist Church since there was no local Friends' Meeting House (church).

Millie and Gerald enjoyed our church but were hesitant to accept our doctrine of baptism. We talked many times, never argued. They were fine Christians, and we knew it. We respected their position. In time, they joined the Valley Baptist Church and were baptized in March 1978. Millie became our Music Director, and Gerald was our treasurer. They moved to the Crusade Church and proved a godsend to them. We loved working with Millie and Gerald Adams.

Steve and Janet Nerger—Crusade's pastor—worked the field in Hazleton and West Hazleton, and the church began to grow. Their tireless efforts and their faithfulness in sharing the Word continued the momentum gained in the crusade. They led the church to buy land and build a beautiful, large church building in a lovely location. That building is a shining tribute to the Nergers and to all the others who sacrificed to build it.

What our neighbors had said wouldn't happen, did happen in a marvelous, inspiring way. Miracle after miracle happened along the way, keeping us ever mindful that it was God's doing, not ours. God continues to bless. He always does when we let him.

The going, knocking on doors, ministering to needs, preaching the Word, teaching observance of all things learned, are all God's commandments. He never fails to honor the keeping of them. One doesn't have to be a Baptist to obey the teachings of the Bible, but any Baptist who doesn't obey is woefully short on commitment. Since we believe we are "a people of the Book," wouldn't it be wonderful if we all acted on that belief?

As mentioned before, it's not an easy life for a pastor and his family in an unevangelized, non-churchgoing part of the country. Your closest pastor friend may live fifty miles away. You may see other Baptists only at associational meetings. Your wife has to work to help supply the needs of the family. Your children have few, or no, Christian friends. It may be difficult for them.

You long to see and be with your aging parents and in-laws who live back in Alabama, Tennessee, Georgia, Mississippi, or wherever you're from. If you are lucky, you see them once a year. Your heart is strained, but your commitment holds. Knowing you have answered *God's call* makes the difference.

What Cornelius and I observed, in twenty-five years of church planting, were that the pastors, who came north to help us start churches, had an unusually high sense of commitment to win people to Christ. They resolved to triumph for the Lord. They came because they saw the need and felt God's call on their lives, to help meet that need. When men and women *know* it is God's call, they can put comforts and pleasures in second, third, or even fourth place. They learn to put God first.

Such a pastor is not perfect, nor are his wife and children. They face the same joys and sorrows, failures and triumphs, temptations and victories that everybody else faces. But oh, the indescribable joy of being where the Lord wants you and doing what he's called you to do. No amount of money, no position, no material gain, no comforts or pleasures in this world can compare with the perfect exhilaration of saying, "Here am I; send me," and mean it!

While we were settling into the routine in Conyngham, and mellowing Hazleton for the crusade, Alona decided to move from Erie to California. She was born in Oakland and had always felt drawn back there. Though we had vacationed in California through the years, that had not been enough for her. She moved to Oakland in 1979 and has lived in the San Francisco Bay area ever since. She taught school at first but dropped out of teaching at one point (1984–1986) to attend Golden Gate Seminary. She received her Master of Religious Education Degree there in 1986. Then she returned to the classroom.

June and Jim had moved from Grand Island, Nebraska, to Pittsburgh. Jim started teaching, and June began working on her Masters in Social Work. Upon getting her Masters, she started working at Saint Francis Hospital but later moved to Allegheny General Hospital.

CHAPTER 6

Building Bridges to Cross Barriers

CONYNGHAM HAD BEEN OUR HOME FOR ABOUT FOUR and a half years when the Missions Committee of the Greater Pittsburgh Baptist Association asked Cornelius to come to Pittsburgh as Church Planter Strategist. This association, made up of nine counties in the southwestern corner of Pennsylvania, had a population of two and a half million people. The job title, Church Planter Strategist, meant a person who could find places churches were needed and execute plans to begin them. Cornelius was gifted in that area.

Tongue in cheek, Cornelius asked me if I'd mind living in the same city with our one and only grandson. Of course he was being facetious! I was overjoyed with the prospect. June and Jim had separated and were in the process of getting a divorce. That was a great heartache for us because we loved them so much. We could not understand why they had taken that path. They remained friends and shared custody of Simon. They lived only a few blocks from each other and both tried very hard to make things as normal as possible for Simon.

We felt the "natural" pull toward Pittsburgh, but, as always, we sought God's will in this decision. We reveled in the miracles of the Hazleton work. They assured us God was still using us to help start churches. You can be happy in your work, even successful by the world's standards, but if God wants you to be somewhere else, doing something else, you'd best talk to him and pack your bags. Our prayers brought a sense of closure to our work in Conyngham. It seemed clear that it was time for us to move to Pittsburgh.

In the spring of 1982, we moved to Raven Drive in Scott Township. It was just outside of Mt. Lebanon city limits which were just outside Pittsburgh city limits. It was good to be near June and Simon, and, as much as possible, we stayed close to Jim.

Excited about his new job, Cornelius went about it enthusiastically. He was encouraged by the churches which shared his vision and dreams for the many underchurched areas of the Greater Pittsburgh area. We were happy in our move.

Pittsburgh is different. It's a city of bridges of every description. At the request of the Pittsburgh Association Woman's Missionary Union (WMU), I wrote a poem called "Bridges." It was used as a handout in the WMU Convention when the Southern Baptist Convention met in Pittsburgh in 1983. Its message speaks volumes to those who believe God can use all of us to cross the barriers between believers and unbelievers. In the light of this poem, it seems it's up to each person to decide to be, or not to be, a bridge.

BRIDGES

Bridges are for crossing
Spaces big and wide,
Or small and narrow,
Anywhere.
Bridges connect places
From here to there,
From there to here
Or yonder.

Bridges are long or short
   High or low
      Thin or fat, arched or flat,
         Ornate or plain.
But every bridge
   Has a purpose.
      It makes the impossible
         Possible.
Are you a bridge?
   Could you be one?
      Could you be a crossing
         Over deep chasms of darkness,
            Over shallow creeks of prejudice,
            Over wide expanses
               Of indifference
                  And Self-indulgence?
Could you be the bridge
   From hate to love,
      From ignorance to knowledge,
      To JESUS!
Could you be
   The long bridge that brings joy
      Where there is despair?
   The short bridge that brings healing
      Where there is pain?
   The high bridge that brings humility
      Where there is pride?
   The low bridge that brings acceptance
      Where there is self-destruction?
   The thin bridge that brings nurturing
      Where there is want?
   The fat bridge that brings sharing
      Where there is affluence?
   The arched bridge that brings appreciation
      Where there is cultural bias?
   The ornate bridge that brings beauty
      Where there is ugliness?

> The plain bridge that brings TRUTH
> Where there is confusion?
> A bridge makes it possible
> To get where you are not—
> Through love, through knowledge, through JESUS!

If you've never been to Pittsburgh, you can't conceive the endless array of bridges. If you've ever lived there, you can't forget them. They didn't intimidate Cornelius. He took to Pittsburgh like a duck takes to water. He was invigorated by the challenge of each new place/church he had to find. The ups and downs, the overs and unders, and even the throughs (tunnels) were fun for him.

But for me? Frankly, I was glad we bought a house out in Scott Township, where the bridges were fewer, and the hills weren't so high and rugged. I marvelled constantly that so many lanes of city traffic could merge and diverge successfully, with everybody in a hurry. I credit Pittsburgh drivers with outstanding courtesy and *nerve*. I've never seen more considerate drivers. Of course, there, your life depended on it!

We loved Pittsburgh. Years before, when we were in Warren, Ohio, we worked with the Pittsburgh Baptist Association. We gained strength and friendship from the churches as we were able to attend associational meetings. Also, I took my sixth graders every year on field trips to the Planetarium, the Aviary, museums, and parks in Pittsburgh. We even occasionally attended ball games at Three Rivers Stadium.

However, to live in such a city is different from visiting there. We found it most exhilarating. We marvelled at much of what we saw of this highly cultural city. And we adored being near June and Simon. But all of those good things were not the reason for our moving to Pittsburgh.

We didn't forget our purpose—to start churches. We joined the Mt. Lebanon Baptist Chapel but were seldom there for the morning service. We were out getting acquainted with the people in the churches. However, we always tried to get back for the evening service. Some of the best friends we ever made were in the Mt. Lebanon Chapel. We treasured those days together and felt God had a purpose for all of us being there—at that time.

Something connected to our work, which gave us great pleasure through the years, was working with the summer missionaries sent by the Home Mission Board to help in new work areas. They enjoyed the little "extras" we provided. In Erie we'd go to Niagara Falls and over into Canada. When we were in Warren, Ohio, we'd take them to a ball game in Cleveland. In northeastern Pennsylvania (Conyngham), we'd go the Pocono Mountains, or to visit Harrisburg, the state capital, or even to Philadelphia.

In Pittsburgh, there were so many choices! I think the thing the summer workers, and we, enjoyed most was Point State Park, where the Ohio and the Allegheny Rivers come together. It was in downtown Pittsburgh. We'd take a picnic supper, sprawl on the grass, and listen to marvelous concerts. Oh, what fun that was!

The Associational Missions Committee asked us to start a church and let them observe our approach to church planting. The opportunity soon presented itself. Bill Crowe, pastor of the Expressway Baptist Church, asked Cornelius to preach on Sunday morning about the need for more churches. The story that follows is one I wrote recounting that church start. It was published in *Missions Mosaic* in July 1996.

A CHURCH FOR DENISE

The worship service had ended and people were beginning to leave. An eager young woman, with two preschoolers, approached my husband who had been guest speaker that morning. "Reverend Bright," she said, "why don't we start a church in my community? I drive fifteen miles to attend here. I want my children in church, but it's hard to get here for Sunday

School. We need a church nearer my home."

My husband, Cornelius, said, "We need to talk about that. When can we meet?"

"I'm living with my parents," Denise said. "I'll check with them and call you."

Denise called that afternoon and made an appointment for Thursday. We arrived and found Denise's parents cordial, but her father, Bill, explained, "We have our own church, so we won't be in your Bible study. You're welcome to use our home to teach whoever comes."

We accepted Bill's offer and began that night with an introduction to Bible study. The next week Bill greeted us with, "You're not like we thought you would be. You're just using the Bible in the study."

"Of course, Bill," Cornelius responded. "The Bible is our textbook. What did you expect?"

"We've heard a lot about Southern Baptists," Bill explained. "I suspect we've been getting wrong information." From then on, they never missed Bible study and were the first to join when the church organized.

Three weeks into the Thursday night meetings, I said, "The children and I will go to the family room. I have activities they will enjoy while you study." Four sets of eager feet joined me as we traipsed downstairs.

Soon we were looking for a place for Sunday worship services. We found one, but the Zoning Board refused our request. The chairman suggested we check with the School Board for a building in the same area. Cornelius said, "I've not had much success getting school buildings for church services."

The chairman insisted, "Tell the School Board president I sent you. Maybe he can help."

The next morning, Cornelius met with the School Board president. He was receptive to the idea. He gave us free use of the Stewart School auditorium and any classrooms we needed for Sunday School. Our only expense was to pay the custodian for his time.

Ronnie and Sharon Burkett, pastor of Lower Burrell Baptist Church, with Michelle and Ron.

For a year we drove twenty-eight miles to Lower Burrell for Sunday School and Worship Services. We visited in the community during the week, found opportunities for ministry, and helped the church become known and recognized. The church grew and stabilized. It soon needed a full-time pastor and program.

God called Ronnie and Sharon Burkett, of Louisville, Kentucky, to be the pastor. (Ronnie was one of our 1967 summer missionaries, and he came back in the summer of 1968 to lead our Oil City work.) Their family came ready to work. The church moved from the school building to a house they bought. They also obtained property on which to build. Plans for a building soon materialized.

"It's never been easy," Ronnie explained, "but it's always been rewarding. God didn't call us here to grow a big church. He called us to be faithful in presenting the gospel. As we do that, through preaching and ministry, he grows the church."

The beautiful Lower Burrell Baptist Church building is a testimony to the faith, hard work, difficult times, and financial crunches the members experienced in building it. It is even more a testimony to the love God has for his faithful people. Sometimes, when paths seem darkest, God's light breaks through and is shed abroad. To share in that light is dream fulfillment for pastors and church planters. What an affirmation it is to know that, try as he will, the devil can't defeat God's people when they have a vision and follow him.

While Lower Burrell Church was emerging, Cornelius scouted out other places to begin Bible studies. He visited with pastors to encourage their involvement and input for targeted areas. As he found people willing to have Bible studies in their homes, he initiated the work. The thousands of people in Pittsburgh, who had no church affiliation or preference, made it a ripe mission field. Indeed, many fields were "white unto harvest."

Still, need is not the only criteria for starting a church. Since we Baptists want everyone in the world to hear the gospel, one might think *need* is the only prerequisite to starting a church. But that's not true. Other factors play into the process and must be considered: such things as sponsorship and finances.

Sometimes churches, which might otherwise be sponsors, are burdened with building programs or other worthy projects that take their time, energy, and money. At other times, a young, struggling congregation can't envision a new church start being viable, in the light of their own problems. And to be honest, there is an occasional non-cooperative pastor. Most of the pastors we knew were deeply committed to extending the Kingdom, but they, having had to take secular work to provide for their families, were limited in the time and energy they could give to help start a new work.

Needless to say, young churches are not able to provide full support for their pastor and his family. They have to grow to that point. Even with Church Pastoral Aid (CPA) from the State Convention and Home Mission Board, often the pastor's wife must go to work to help provide the necessities for the family. She would much rather be home, caring for the children and helping her husband in ministry, but the bills have to be paid.

Once an underchurched (or unchurched) place is found, the next steps are carefully considered. Many of these are decided on the basis of a windshield survey (drive through) of the community. In this effort, we discover: 1) kinds of homes, old, new, large, small; 2) families, older, younger, singles; 3) churches in immediate area, kind, and size; 4) nearby shopping areas; 5) general financial level of residents; and 6) community parks and schools.

The most important thing you discover, early on, and this not by a windshield survey, is the availability of a core family where you can have Bible study. Are there homes where Backyard Bible Clubs would be welcomed? Is there a park, or recreation center, where young people can be reached for VBS and ministry opportunities?

Before action is taken on a new start, one must believe, completely, that the Lord is leading in that direction. If there is not that conviction, the project should be delayed. With people praying for the targeted area, God will give a sense of rightness about it, if it's to be pursued. Demographics are important, but God's leadership is more so. If there is a sponsoring church, its Mission Committee will lead out in promoting and supporting the new work.

When the need and prayer support have meshed, door-to-door surveys can begin. If a core family doesn't already exist, you begin cultivating the people to find one who would allow a Bible study in his/her home. One home, with a believing family, can get the work going. When you establish a regular, consistent Bible study time with this core family, the door is opened wide to a new church possibility. As neighbors and friends join the Bible study, the nucleus is being formed.

As interest increases, BBC and VBS can be planned. These initial activities build support that will someday be the foundation for a new church. Finding and meeting ministry needs in the community helps the residents know your commitment is firm, and your concern is real. Sports and other activities for the youth show them you are interested in the whole family. You're making a statement of genuine interest in the community, and you've come to stay. You want to start a church that preaches the Bible and ministers to the needs of the people.

Extending the Kingdom is every Christian's job. Not all are church planters or pastors. God gives all believers gifts to be used in serving him. We do that by serving his people. Wherever we live, as believers, we are to help build the church. If we live where churches are plentiful and needs are being met, we need to reach out to new areas and help in starting still other churches.

While some Christians can give large sums of money to the work, others give their mite. Some can go physically and help do surveys, VBS, BBC, revivals, concerts, work on church buildings; others can stay home and pray. It's not out-of-line to suggest that some could move to new work areas and plant their lives, alongside the missionary family, and serve the Lord. Many jobs are transferable, often with higher pay schedules.

The Holy Spirit leads us to pray for those who go out to preach the Word. He encourages us to pray for those who hear the Word. God forbid that we neglect to pray.

CHAPTER 7

He Did What He Could

THINGS WERE GOING WELL IN THE PITTSBURGH BAPTIST Association and several promising places were found to start Bible studies. Praxis Teams were alerted (seminary couples who go into new work areas to lead beginning churches). Cornelius was never happier in his work.

In early April 1984, my brother, R. C., called me to come home to help him and Chester, my other brother, get Mother reconciled to going into a nursing home. Mother was eighty-four and living alone. We'd tried for years to have someone live with her, but as her health deteriorated, it became harder to do. It worked only part of the time, and never really well.

While I was home with Mother, Cornelius discovered a fist-sized lump in his right side. It would not go away. He saw his internist, Dr. Yeasted, who had, just a month before his sixty-fifth birthday, given him a clean bill of health. That report was so good the Home Mission Board extended his appointment beyond the normal retirement age.

Dr. Yeasted found not only the lump Cornelius found, but another one on the opposite side, on the transverse colon. He said surgery must be done as soon as arrangements could be made—the sooner the better.

96

Not knowing any of this, I stayed in Albertville to get Mother settled in the nursing home. I returned to Pittsburgh on April 25. The surgery was on the 27.

The operation entailed removing eighteen inches of the large colon (both lumps were malignant) and reconnecting it. No colostomy was needed. Dr. Perry, the surgeon, told us the cancer had spread to the peritoneum (membrane lining the abdominal cavity). We knew, from that instant, it was terminal.

Dr. Perry said he would recommend chemotherapy, but since the cancer cells were so widespread, he didn't know if they could be stopped. A fine Christian doctor, Dr. Perry put his hand on Cornelius's shoulder and said with great compassion, "Mr. Bright, you'll have maybe six months to get everything done. Let's hope this cancer doesn't go to the bone. Good luck and God bless you."

Cornelius's recovery from the surgery was rapid. What a paradox! He was physically strong and in "excellent" health, except he was dying with colon cancer. We were aware of hundreds of prayers on our behalf at that time. We know they

Cornelius at home in Pittsburgh.

helped us. We benefited from a great outpouring of love and concern for us from the Pittsburgh churches and individuals. What a lift it was to our broken hearts to know friends all over the country were praying for us.

June and John had planned to be married on May 26—one month from Cornelius's surgery. Now they were hesitating. Cornelius insisted they go on with their plans. He promised not only to attend the wedding, but he'd give June away. And he did, though he was thin, gaunt, and weak.

On the days Cornelius took chemotherapy, his strength was almost nil. When he got over that, he'd feel reasonably well for several days, until the next treatment. During this time, he became interim pastor at the South Park Baptist Church, the church that sponsored us in Erie. He loved it and worked as God gave him strength.

We had a World Mission Conference (WMC) scheduled in late October in Marshall County, Alabama, (our home). We bravely went. Everything went well in the WMC. We enjoyed the fellowship of people we hadn't seen for years. We soaked up all the good things people said to us and about us—things that really helped in the days that followed.

We'd planned a week of vacation to follow the WMC. The day after the conference ended, Cornelius began a siege of diarrhea that lasted eight days. Our vacation was spent at Mother's house, just being quiet, prayerful, and hopeful. We flew back to Pittsburgh on November 9. The diarrhea stopped on November 11.

Almost at once, Cornelius began to blow up like a balloon. He went from a thirty-four-inch waist to forty-two and a half inches. The distention of his abdomen caused great discomfort, and his weight soared to 179 pounds. We knew most of that was fluid. Chemotherapy was stopped and he entered the hospital. Dr. Perry drew off a gallon of fluid and gave Cornelius a shot directly into the abdomen. He hoped the rest of the fluid would leave the body through the natural routes.

After three days in the hospital, Cornelius came home. He'd lost down to 155 pounds. He went back to work, wanting to do what he could, as long as he could. It was during those anxious days and weeks we repeated so often to our friends, and to ourselves, "We don't know what the future holds for us, but we know *who* holds the future. We are not afraid."

Alona came home for Christmas. We rejoiced she'd made plans to stay with us through January. June, John, Simon, and Jim were most supportive during those uncertain months. It was wonderful being near them.

How hard it is to experience the emotional roller coaster of a terminal illness. For patient and caregiver, every breath is filled with hope and despair. There's never a moment, or thought, free of the disease. *It's just there!* But even closer to the heart than the devastating disease is the undaunting assurance that God is also there. Where else can one go when all earth's efforts fail? The Christian goes to God and, in the stillness, knows he is right there with him/her. Cornelius and I knew God never left us, nor forsook us, even for one moment.

Many friends, who commiserated with me, asked how I could handle losing Cornelius and still have an upbeat attitude. My reply to them, and to all who wonder why good people suffer and die, is Isaiah 57:1–2:

> The righteous perish, and no one ponders it in his heart; devout men are taken away, and no one understands that the righteous are taken away to be spared from evil. Those who walk uprightly enter into peace; they find rest as they lie in death.

No, I don't know why Cornelius had cancer and had to die, but I praise the Lord for sparing him whatever evil lurked in his path. How merciful our God is! How he loves us, and how patient he is with our slowness to comprehend his ways.

We had known, from the beginning, that Cornelius's life would be limited in time. Six months, Dr. Perry had told us. He told me to help Cornelius do whatever he wanted to get done as quickly as possible. The six months was only a guess.

From the beginning, Cornelius and I talked openly about what was happening to him. We were grateful for that precious time. We recounted our successes and our failures, our joys and our sorrows, our hopes and our dreams. We spent many hours remembering God's goodness and mercy. We had no reason to doubt him now. We cheered each other by talking about Alona, June, John, Simon, and Jim. We loved them and wanted only the best for them. We were very proud of our little family. How sad it was for Cornelius to leave them.

We reminisced about the work God had called us to do and the great people we'd met along the way. We fully accepted the fact that our future would be brief, but as God had been with us in the past, we knew he was certainly with us now and would be in the future. I wish every couple could have that kind of closure when life is limited because death is approaching. I know some people can't accept that approach to death, but it was wonderful for Cornelius and me.

Wisdom told us it was time to put our house on the market. With Alona home to help us, we made preparations to sell the house and move back to Albertville, Alabama. It was hard leaving the work we'd felt called to do. It was hard to admit that, even though Dr. Perry's six-month prediction had been exceeded, time was running out.

The house sold, and Cornelius and I, surrounded at the airport by a loving group of pastors and friends, boarded a plane for home. Alona drove our car, and Tommy Calhoun, our nephew, drove the furniture truck and pulled our Chevette behind it. Margaret Washington, our niece, met our plane in Birmingham and drove us to Albertville. Before we even reached the house, Cornelius insisted we go by the nursing home and see Mother. It was January 24, her eighty-fifth birthday. Cornelius loved Mother very much, and I think he thought he would never see her again. He didn't.

We made an appointment at Montclair Hospital in Birmingham for Cornelius to see Dr. Waid Shelton, a friend from our Birmingham days when we lived next door to his grandparents. We knew Cornelius's days were fast dwindling, but we wanted the best possible care for him. We had that in Waid Shelton.

On Sunday morning, February 24—one month to the day after our arrival back in Alabama, Cornelius died at Montclair Hospital. His homegoing was peaceful and welcomed. It was as if he did, in death, what he had done as a pastor-missionary for years. He arose early, about 5:00 A.M., to meet his Lord, to go over the Scripture and notes he'd planned to use in his sermon that day. What a thought!

The funeral was a celebration of Cornelius's life, just as he'd wanted it to be. He did what he could, as long as he could. I'm convinced he heard, "Well done, thou good and faithful servant."

Alona and June stayed a few days to help do the many things that have to be done after a funeral. And, of course, to comfort me. Most Christians know the pain of separation is eased only by the knowledge that death is not the end. It's only a transition, and someday we'll see our loved ones again.

The days following the funeral were filled with visits and messages from friends across the country. I shall never forget the marvelous calming effect Annis Nelson's visit had on my heart. I don't remember a word she said. I just remember her comforting presence. It was much like that of the Lord. Thank you, Annis.

Twenty-five years of church planting ended for me with Cornelius's death. What would I do now? I needed to stay in Albertville to minister to Mother in the nursing home. That was a wise decision because in October that year, my brother, R. C., died, leaving me as Mother's sponsor and bill payer. I am so glad I was here to be that.

I've traveled a lot to speak and teach on missions, led programs, attended conferences, participated in World Mission Conferences, and been active in my home church. As Mother's health declined, I spent more time with her. Those were precious hours. Near the end, Mother spoke of her childhood and people I'd never heard of before, but it was so healing for me to see her precious smiles when she talked of by-gone days. Mother died on January 3, 1990—just twenty-one days before her ninetieth birthday.

I visited Alona, in California, and June, in Pittsburgh. I was able to be with June when her second son, John Albert, was born, just as I had been with her when Simon Brook was born, fourteen years before.

For a couple of years I managed the Martling Nutrition Center. That was fun, and I loved the people, but I just needed to get on with my lifelong dream—writing.

I took a writing course to learn how to write well enough to write this book. Once more, the Lord has permitted my dream to come true. It is written. My prayer is that all who read it will see God's triumphant, guiding hand in the lives of countless ordinary people. And, in seeing, will make themselves available to God.

There is no doubt God uses ordinary people. Just look at Cornelius and me! I'm so glad he used us to plant churches. To him be the glory, great things he has done!